The Fall of Tsingtao

The Fall of Tsingtao

EDWIN P. HOYT

Arthur Barker Limited London
A subsidiary of Weidenfeld (Publishers) Limited

Contents

Acknowledgements

The background of Tsingtao and German colonial history comes from several sources, notably, *Tsingtao Under Three Flags*, by Wilson Leon Godshall, published by the Commercial Press of Shanghai in 1929, and *Das Buch der Deutschen Kolonien*, a compilation of studies of all the colonies with a foreword by Dr Heinrich Schnee, published in Leipzig in 1937.

Der Kreuzerkrieg in den ausländischen Gewässern, by the then Captain Erich Raeder, was useful in telling part of the story of the colony's defence. So was *Japans Seemacht*, by Gustav Jensen, published in Berlin in 1938.

Sir Julian Corbett's *History of the Great War, Naval Operations*, was vital for tracing the activity of the British and Japanese during the early days of the war.

As for the siege itself I relied on a number of sources. In the June 1929 issue of *Proceedings of the United States Naval Institute* Lt Emil B. Perry wrote an account of the *Siege of Tsingtao*. I also made extensive use of the highly romanticized *Von Tsingtao zu den Falklandinseln* by *Fregattenkapitän* Hugo Waldener, published in Berlin in 1917. This was a book written in the heat of war. But it does have much of value in setting scenes in Tsingtao during the siege.

The *Times* of London's *History of the War, Volume II* was interesting and useful, although full of jingoism and lavish praise of the Japanese that seems a bit odd two wars later. If the book overplays Japan at least it did not have the temerity to overdo the British role in Tsingtao – the *Times* was quite restrained and useful in this way. But its inaccuracies about the whole German scene and story are notable.

One basic work on the siege, from the point of view of the Japanese and British, is Jefferson Jones's *The Fall of Tsingtao*, published in Boston in 1915. It is a fine journalistic account of what he saw.

I am grateful to librarians at the US Naval Academy in Annapolis, Md. and at the US Navy library in Washington for use of a great deal of other material. Some of the research for this book was done in connection with *The Last Cruise of the Emden*, which was published in England and the US a number of years ago. Also, earlier I wrote a study of Admiral von Spee and the cruiser squadron which yielded information about Tsingtao in that fateful summer of 1914.

A very interesting article about Gunther Pluschow appeared in the *Cross & Cockade*, the Journal of the Society of World War I Aero Historians, written by John H. Tegler. I am grateful to David Winans of the society for this and other information about the time, place and events.

CHAPTER ONE

The German Colony

As the warming sun of spring came to the German colony of Kiaochow on China's Shantung peninsula in May 1914, there could hardly have been a more peaceful and prosperous place in all of Asia. For the Germans, having found China good to them in terms of exploitation, had done their very best to make a proper German place of the colony and its capital of Tsingtao.

German interest in China came from watching what England, France and Russia were doing in the middle of the nineteenth century. The first treaty, in 1861, provided largely for trade concessions that were more or less equal to those granted the British cousins of Germany. In the next twenty years, Germany expanded her colonial empire in Africa, and the South Seas, and watched affairs in China closely as Japan and the European powers snatched away huge chunks of imperial territory. The German government was eager to have a coaling station for the new fleet that was about to be formed, and German ambassadors travelled to Peking to plead their case. But after the Sino-Japanese war of 1895, the Chinese court was unwilling to make any unforced concessions, so the Germans were turned down. They did not have the naval or military strength in the Far East to push their claim. German traders in Tientsin and Hankow were roughly handled and German ships were refused the niceties.

All this while Britain, France, Russia and China were pushing along with their colonial designs, and luckily for Germany they quarrelled. In the quarrel the Deutsche-Asiatische Bank got its foot in the door of Chinese finances, lending money that was backed by the taxes collected in the Yangtse river valley. Although

A*

Germany still had no colonies in China, she continued to send traders and missionaries to the Far East.

Then came heaven-sent opportunity. Casting about for unoccupied territory on the coast of China, the Germans had looked covetously at Kiaochow bay on the southern coast of Shantung. It was virtually unused, occupied only by a few fishermen, but the bay was a great deep-water port, as fine as any that existed in Asia, well enclosed by good high land.

The opportunity was made by the Chinese themselves, who were rising ever more often in anti-foreign demonstrations as the Europeans seized their lands. One day in November 1897, a Chinese mob murdered two German Roman Catholic missionaries, Franz Nies and Richard Henle. It was just the overt act for which Berlin had been waiting.

In the fuss and bluster that followed, German 'might' won what German 'right' had been denied: a foothold on the Shantung peninsula, which included a ninety-nine-year lease on Kiaochow bay, with a colony extending in a semi-circular curve from the bay with a radius of fifty kilometres from the central point. Altogether the Germans received control of about two hundred square miles. They also secured the right to build a railroad from Tsingtao to Tsinanfu, the Chinese capital of Shantung province, and another to the town of Tschoufu, or Chou-fu. They won important mineral concessions along the right of way – very valuable to them because of the large coal deposits in Shantung.

The Germans determined, then, that they would make their new colony a showplace, and they began spending money. First, in careful Germanic fashion, they surveyed what they had: a peninsula with the village of Tsingtao and a tiny place called Haihsi, plus a few small islands in the bay. From the sea the boundary extended northeast along a mountainous area; the highest peak, Lauting mountain, was 1,130 metres.

Here were their own little alps. Almost immediately the Germans organized an *Alpenverein* and began planning climbs. They would put up hostels and stopping places and turn the

Chinese mountain country into a veritable Bavaria. Much of the area was mountainous and the Germans soon named the mountains for themselves: Prinz Heinrich Peak, Moltke, Bismarck, Diederichs. Obviously all this had little to do with the Chinese, but the Germans were like the other Europeans – they were not joining a civilization, but imposing one atop another.

The Germans then examined the climate in which they found themselves. In the summer, their peninsula was caressed by a warm southern wind, but in winter the blasts from Siberia brought subzero cold. Springtime sometimes also came in with sandstorms from the northwest. In the interior it could become devilishly hot in midsummer, but along the coast it was almost always cool and breezy, so the Germans decided to build seaside resorts in the great halfmoon bay they had seized. Theirs would be the finest, most hygienic foreign colony in all China, they decided.

In the entire colony there were about 100,000 Chinese residents, farmers and fishermen for the most part. The villages were typically Chinese: huts of clay or mud-brick, with roofs of straw or seaweed, and windows of paper. The Germans took a look at the village of Tsingtao, and immediately below it laid out a city of wide streets. They did not tear down the Buddhist and Taoist temples they found in the old city, but they simply avoided the Chinese town and made their own creation.

The first to come to the new colony were the military: a battalion of marines, a field battery and a detachment of a shore battery. The admiralty was in charge of this colonization so far from home, and the chief of the admiralty, Dr Schrameier, warned all who had any ambitions to come to the new colony that what would be expected of them, on behalf of the fatherland, was work, work, and more work.

When the government of the colony was established, it, too, was a typical, efficient German operation. The governor was chief civil administrator, and also commander of the garrison. The civil administration consisted of the courts, the building administration that controlled the planning and erection of every edifice in the new town, the port authority, and an astronomical-meteorological station.

To start from scratch and build a city and colony was not cheap, but the Germans were ready: in the first year Berlin allocated DM 36,000, largely for planning. That was 1899. Then came the actual building; five years later the expenditure was nearly half a million marks, and in 1909 the government spent almost two and a half million marks. By this time Tsingtao, the German city, was a handsomely planned town, complete with German-style buildings, most of them two- and three-storeyed a Protestant church on a broad open green, a Roman Catholic church and monastery, and a bevy of trading establishments.

Most important was the building of the port, which began in 1901. Two moles were to be built within a protective jetty five kilometres around. The work was begun in March and two years later Tsingtao boasted one of the most modern harbours in all Asia, with a tall lighthouse guarding the entrance, and inside a pair of harbours, the big one for the ocean-going vessels of the Germans and other Europeans, and, a little to the southwest, a small harbour for the Chinese junks and sampans.

By this time European and Chinese cities were entirely separated. Thirty thousand Chinese lived in their own town, behind the western city. Below them, on the bay, lived the Europeans, boasting of their 'artistic culture city' that would last for ever, because every building was constructed to stand for at least a hundred years.

The Germans traded with the Chinese, of course. They brought in cotton manufactured goods, chemicals, and metal manufactures. They took out Chinese art, cereals, raw cotton, tobacco, beans, potatoes, and peanuts. The colony was not nearly so important a trading adjunct of the homeland as were the African colonies, for example, but it had its vital place in Germany's insistence that she be numbered among the great powers of the world.

By 1910 Germany had planted her foot firmly in this faraway

place, and many people from the fatherland were happily making their lives there. They were also bringing a taste of western culture to the Chinese that was not very typical of Europeans. They built a brickyard, and hired Chinese labourers to make bricks. That was certainly in the western character. But they also brought in machinery and established machine shops, and then built a technical middle school and taught Chinese youths to become machinists. They established printing firms and published a newspaper and books. They examined silkworm culture and added western production methods as far as they could.

The thoroughness with which the Germans built indicated the depth of their national desire to remain a part of this China of theirs. The railroad moved steadily westwards – to Weihsien in 1902, to Tsotien in 1903, to Tsinanfu in 1904, and by 1910 the stations had been built and the line was running busily. This development was really important, for a great value of the colony to Germany was the coal supply. The railroad brought out 126,000 tons of coal in 1909 – a fact that was not lost on the Japanese who had long wanted the Shantung peninsula and its resources for their own. Coal-starved Japan looked hungrily on the German efforts, and waited.

Schools were raised as the Germans settled in; government schools for the German young, divided at the upper level into young men's and young women's institutions. The missions ran schools for the Chinese. Dr Wunsch also established the mission hospital for the Ostasien-Mission, which had its Asian headquarters in Tsingtao, and here he ran a clinic for the poor Chinese.

The military did not rule with a heavy hand, although Kiaochow was very much a military colony. During the Boxer troubles, two companies of the *III Seebataillon* made the long march from Tientsin to Peking with the Seymour expedition, but this was a part of the general foreign presence in China. In the later years the troops stayed mostly in their own bailiwick, policing the colony without much trouble; guarding the railroad, the mountain works, and the missions.

As the Germans came and built the railroad, the port facilities and the town, they put up clubs and restaurants, theatres and other places of entertainment. They built a polo field and a racecourse on the edge of the town. By 1914, less than twenty years after the German presence was established in China, the Germans had settled in and Tsingtao had become notable as the summer place for foreigners. Englishmen from Hong Kong and the Yangtse valley and Frenchmen from Yunnan and even Indo-China came up to enjoy the beaches and the rounds of entertainment that seemed to know very little nationalism in these happy days. Many a young German naval officer, posted to Kiaochow for a stay of three or four years, found it hard and upsetting to go home, so pleasant was the life of the European in Asia.

CHAPTER TWO

The Admiralty's Plan

As far as the German Admiralty was concerned in the ten years before the beginning of the Great War, Kiaochow was to serve as the major imperial naval base for operations that would be carried out against the European enemies in Far Eastern waters.

A navy Germany would have – that much was decided by Count von Bismarck and his minions. But what kind of a navy, and for what purpose – those were matters that kept the world and the Reichstag debating for many a month at the turn of the century. There would be a challenge of Britain's naval might, and to make it the Germans developed the *Hochseeflotte*. But as a power that counted its borders primarily on land, Germany did not have the resources to put battleships and big cruisers everywhere round the world. So the admiralty developed and the Reichstag accepted the theory of the light cruiser force. A light cruiser was big enough to show the flag in any foreign clime, yet was small enough that the government could afford to spread a little in the number to be built. These ships should be very useful in case of war; war could be with England, and the little cruisers could raid the seven seas, cutting England off from her colonies and starving her into submission. This policy was not arrived at easily or lightly, but it was a logical policy for a power whose strength lay mainly on the land, and by 1914 it was the policy of the German naval authority.

As far as Tsingtao was concerned, its main line of defence was the cruiser squadron. It was not envisaged that a war in Europe would be fought on land in Asia. The squadron and its support ships should be able to protect the colony from any normal danger that could be foreseen.

Thus, in spite of the organization tables laid out in the beginning when Shantung was colonized by the Germans, the most
important figure in Tsingtao was not the governor, but the
commander of the cruiser squadron. There was no doubt about
it, their names and ranks told the story. The commandant of the
garrison was *Kapitän-zur-See* Meyer-Waldeck, a full captain
in the Imperial navy and thus a man of importance. But the
commander of the German cruiser squadron was the Graf von
Spee, a vice-admiral in the navy, and several of his officers were
superior in service to Captain Meyer-Waldeck.

Early in 1914 back in Berlin there were feelings of unrest in
the political circles of the capital. There was nothing new about
these; diplomats were forever speculating on what might happen
in the world under conditions X, Y, or Z. And yet no military
authority worth its salt could fail to keep aware of rumours and
stories that involved serious international dealings. So the admiralty was aware, and there were constant stirrings in the war
plans department.

In spite of the extensive empire the Germans had managed to
acquire in the last quarter of the nineteenth century, the
admiralty's basic war plan had to be concerned with the defence
of waterways around Germany herself, and with the press of operations against foreign commerce. Still, every conceivable war plan
took into account the various conditions and missions of the colonies, and Kiaochow, the China colony, had its role in them all.

Kriegsfall B envisaged war against France and Russia, with
Germany fighting alone and England neutral. In that case, there
would be very little to worry about in Tsingtao, and the
Kreuzergeschwader – cruiser squadron – could concentrate on the
destruction of the French and the Russian shipping that worked
out of Vladivostok.

Kriegsfall C envisaged war against England. In this case, the
squadron would head towards the west coast of America and
operate in the Pacific. If need be the Netherlands Indies could
be used for coaling stations.

Kriegsfall B und C foresaw war against France, Russia and England. This, of course, meant the Australian navy would be involved and that was important because of the German colonies in Samoa and New Guinea. In this case, Admiral von Spee's squadron would carry on cruiser warfare in the East Asian waters against the ships of all these nations. 'Cruiser warfare' to the Germans had a special meaning: the word *Kreuzerkrieg* signified the kind of warfare that in a later time would be carried out by submarines. But in early 1914 the submarine was not considered by naval authorities to be nearly so significant a weapon as it would become within the year. The light cruiser was the weapon of chase; it could overhaul any merchant steamer and could outgun anything but a heavy or armoured cruiser. Thus the light cruiser and the auxiliary cruiser were to be Germany's principal weapons in East Asian waters, come war.

All plans had one big question mark built in: in case of war what was Japan going to do?

For the past few years the Germans had spent a considerable amount of money and much persuasiveness in the hope that the Japanese government would remain neutral in case of a war in Europe. Yet Berlin was aware of the Anglo-Japanese alliance that called for mutual aid. And it was apparent that from Japan's point of view the Anglo-Japanese alliance had been constructed to protect Japanese interests against the only two powers that might threaten her: Russia and Germany. The threat of Germany was far more remote than that of Russia, but the Germans were astute enough to recognize the reality: every one of their war plans raised the question of Japan, although none answered it very well.

So in the spring of 1914, when the time came to rotate a part of the garrison at Tsingtao, the Hamburg-Amerika liner *Patricia* was dispatched from Wilhelmshaven bearing all the supplies necessary to augment the defence of the colony, and dispatches for Admiral von Spee and Captain Meyer-Waldeck that indicated the general unrest in Europe. She also bore a

number of men destined for the cruiser squadron, to replace
sailors whose enlistments had run out, and officers for squadron
and garrison, including a brand new Rumpler Taube two-place
monoplane, which was to become the garrison's air force.

No one in the admiralty was looking for war that summer,
but it was the task of the naval authority to be prepared for any
eventuality.

CHAPTER THREE

Glorious Tsingtao

One brilliant day in May 1914, as the wispy white clouds hung motionless in the still air above Tsingtao, there arrived at the big grey administration building *Leutnant-zur-See* Gunther Pluschow of His Majesty's Imperial Navy, with the astounding news that he was to establish an air force as part of the East Asia squadron.

Captain Meyer-Waldeck was surprised, for *Leutnant* Pluschow had beaten his orders; he had come overland on the Trans-Siberian railroad from Germany to the station, while his airplane and all the information was coming aboard the *Patricia* along with the replacements and supplies for the cruiser squadron.

But Meyer-Waldeck was an urbane and gracious officer, so the surprise did not keep him from offering friendship and hospitality to the new addition to Kiaochow colony's naval garrison. They chatted for a while, and then *Leutnant* Pluschow was dismissed to set up in his quarters and visit the officers' club that would become the centre of his social existence in this very social place.

As the young man left, Meyer-Waldeck shook his head slowly, for in these modern times events were moving almost past belief. The governor had known Pluschow's father; he too had been a naval man, and it was always a tight little service. But for young Gunther to come to him with an airplane virtually in hand was an indication of the headlong rush of the twentieth century.

Young Pluschow was, indeed, the most modern of naval figures. He had begun life as a cadet, and served on the four-masted training ships which taught young men to freeze and slave on the icy wooden decks in the gales of the North Sea. He had become a line officer and had worked his way up to be a

full two-striper. Then Gunther Pluschow had been bitten by the
aviation bug, and when the admiralty decided to venture into
the aviation experiment and formed its naval air service, he was
one of the earliest applicants.

Pluschow went to school again. He learned what little the
experts had to teach him on the ground, and then went into the
air. After two lessons he soloed. Two days later he had done all
that was required, learned all that anyone at the station could
teach him, and was pronounced an airman. He was obviously one
of those remarkable men like Baron von Richthofen, having that
genius for flying.

In 1913 Pluschow perfected his cross-country flying technique,
going up in every kind of plane that he could put his hands on.
He practised altitude flying too, and assisted Herr Linnekogel in
an attempt to wrest the altitude record from the French, which
Linnekogel did with a flight that reached 5,500 metres. By this
time Pluschow himself was becoming well known in German
air circles. Then came the spring of 1914, and the assignment
to the China station, which offered all kinds of excitement and
adventure.

Now, dismissed by Captain Meyer-Waldeck to check in at the
officers' club and get to know the city, Pluschow took a rickshaw
and began to look around him.

He went down to the harbour, and there he saw lying before
him the result of the German government's impressive work of
the past fifteen years. The big circular jetty provided fifteen
thousand feet of breakwater that enclosed the harbour on two
sides, protecting it from the northwest winds that came howling
down out of Mongolia. On the third side the mountains protected
the haven, and the land jutted out between the city and the
eastern side of the peninsula that had made the natural harbour
of Kiaochow bay.

The south side of the harbour was the wharf side, and here
were the two points in which Pluschow was immediately interested. First was the long shipping dock, with its 2,500-foot

wharf and three rail lines that could handle half a dozen ships at once. That is where *Patricia* would come in, bringing the Rumpler.

Five hundred feet away stood the naval wharf, with its three warehouses, or godowns as they were called in Asia, and its four rail spurs. This was the property of the German East Asia squadron, and here the ships came to load and fit and arm. At this moment in harbour were the gunboat *Tiger*, the big cruisers *Scharnhorst* and *Gneisenau*, the light cruiser *Leipzig*, the torpedo boat *S-90*, and a number of colliers and other supply ships. The remainder of the squadron was scattered about the Pacific on various bits of His Majesty's business, from showing the flag in Japan, to patrolling the Yangtse river against pirates and the unruly warlords who had the idea that the Chinese should conquer China.

Across the hill from the harbour, Pluschow could see the Chinese city, Taitungchen, which drew more people every year as the German colony grew prosperous in its trade of silks and precious goods and raw materials, and its growth of manufactures that were helping to supply the homeland with Oriental goods.

Along the beach of the outer harbour Pluschow could also see the grey and white and red-tiled roofs of the big houses of the colonial officials and the business people. On the hillside above the city lay the garrison, showing its force to all who looked, rising above even the slender tower of the Evangelical *Kirche*. Off to one side he saw the rust and paint and miscellaneous parts that denoted the repair harbour with its dry dock. And beyond were the picturesque sampans and junks, with their Chinese families scurrying about the vessels, living their mysterious lives.

It was certainly hilly country, Pluschow noted, without a great deal of satisfaction. For his problem was to keep going one cranky little airplane, without access to a machine shop designed for aircraft, and without a great number of spare parts. His first problem was to get his plane. His second was to find a place to fly it.

He returned from the harbour to the town, marvelling at the lindens and the other trees that reminded him so much of home, and at the broad streets, forty feet wide with enormous pavements. At a pinch one could land the Rumpler in the middle of the city.

Pluschow wandered about, looking over the Chinese temples that contrasted so brightly with the staid burgher architecture that might have been in Darmstadt. He visited the country club, and the famous Dachsal restaurant where the sea captains hung out, but what excited him most was the racecourse. For if he could secure the permission of the governor, there was his aviation field, all built and ready for him. And why not? He could certainly schedule his flying time so it would not interfere with the races.

For the next month, Pluschow did very little but familiarize himself with the city and the colony, and engage in the play that was so great a part of colonial life. He was waiting for his airplane and for the two captive balloons and the petty officer and men of the air service who had been assigned to his detachment, but who were coming with the equipment on the *Patricia*.

Pluschow went to the officers' club and there he met and was befriended by the young lieutenants and commanders of the squadron, some of whom he knew from old days on the training ship, some from previous assignments. He met *Oberleutnant-zur-See* Georg von Plissow, first officer of the *Tiger*, an officer in his late twenties. He met Plissow's twin brother Hans, also *Oberleutnant* who was posted ashore in charge of an artillery unit. Pluschow and Hans von Plissow had a good deal in common, for Hans had trained at Johannisthal for his pilot's licence, and at the time that Pluschow arrived Hans was designated as air officer, for whatever good that did him. Hans had hoped to be the airman of the station, until Pluschow showed up.

Pluschow also met *Oberleutnants* Berg and Heistermann of the big cruiser *Gneisenau*, *Oberleutnant* Bornhuber from the *Leipzig*, and *Oberleutnant* Bronner, a Hamburg man, who commanded the torpedo boat *S-90*. There were also two artillery officers from the fortress, *Oberleutnants* Schwartmann and Falck.

The young men soon showed Lieutenant Pluschow the special ropes of Tsingtao. There was as much of the high life as he cared to have, from tennis parties at the country club, to balls at the governor's mansion, a day at the racecourse, or the mountains to climb. There were teas and picnics and meals at the restaurants, staged by Chinese functionaries. For the Germans got on well with their Chinese host-slaves; they had the good sense early on to turn over the functioning of the colony to the Chinese, so in many cases all but the top officials of the administrative departments were Chinese. Thus the administration ran smoothly from a western standpoint, although in ways that the Europeans gave little pretence of understanding.

And so the long weeks passed, until finally in the middle of June, *Patricia* was announced by Radio Tsingtao, the huge transmitting and receiving station on the hill that could send radiograms as far as the South Seas. At last she had arrived and so had the precious Rumpler Taube.

CHAPTER FOUR

Clouds of War

From the quay the assembled troops of the German garrison at
Tsingtao could see the *Patricia* as she rounded the corner and
moved past Cape Jatan which guards the harbour from the open
sea. She came in, flags flying and smoke trailing her, surrounded
by a bevy of harbour boats that sped back and forth and around
in circles like porpoises at play.

As the ship drew in the naval band struck up its military music
and the crowd on the quay began to cheer and wave. To all the
world it would seem that it was a holiday, and indeed that is
precisely the case, for every Relief Day was a holiday in
Tsingtao. It was the official welcoming of the forces from home,
but also on the ship would be travellers who had spent a few
months in Germany on business, and relatives who were coming
to the colony to visit, or to stay. There were brides and grooms
and new businessmen as well as the naval officers and ratings who
would replace those leaving in a few days.

Aboard the ships in harbour, the officers and men were
dressed in their formal white uniforms, standing at attention as
the *Patricia* came in. Admiral von Spee was on the bridge of the
Scharnhorst, his squadron flagship, and those who knew his
small spare figure could spot the telltale goatee and moustache.
Next to him stood his two sons, both lieutenants in the navy and
both his aides.

The bands played, the flags flew, the *Patricia* dipped her
ensign, and all the while she moved slowly, majestically alongside
the big, long quay where the people stood and waited.

Then the steamer blew her blast of greeting, the lines and
cables were made fast, the gangplank came up, and the people

began going ashore, to be greeted with handclasps and embraces by their friends and loved ones. In an hour the troops were moving out to barracks in an orderly fashion, and the Chinese stevedores were bringing the cargo down in nets and out in boxes and barrels to the godowns. The harbour quietened, and the festivity moved to the city, to its clubs and private homes and restaurants. And at the end of the evening, it was agreed by all that never had Relief Day been more joyous, never had the future seemed so bright. Except that in his house ashore, Admiral von Spee was reading telegrams from Berlin that indicated even more unrest than usual, and as far as he was concerned there was something definitely in the air, an uneasiness it was hard to define from so far away.

The admiral considered his force and his responsibilities. His area of responsibility was huge. It included all of Asia, the western coast of the Americas, the Indian Ocean as far as Madagascar, down to the Antarctic. To serve this area he had but a handful of ships. There were the two big cruisers *Scharnhorst* and *Gneisenau,* then the light cruisers *Leipzig, Dresden, Nürnburg* and *Emden.* Besides these ships there were three old vessels, the *Condor, Geier* and *Cormoran* in southern areas. To aid in the policing of the Yangtse and the other dangerous Chinese waters, he had the old gunboats *Iltis, Jaguar, Luchs, Tiger* and *Eber.* Then, working in and out of Tsingtao were the gunboats *Otter* and *Tsingtao,* and the survey ship *Planet* in the South Seas, plus old *S-90,* that might or might not be able to get out of Tsingtao harbour when the time came.

On the face of it, this was a formidable force, but many of these vessels were so old as to be useless except against colonials. When it came down to modern military action, the admiral had his cruiser squadron and very little else to protect the German interest in almost half the world.

The summer, with all its uncertainties, also held many responsibilities for Admiral von Spee. It was time to show the flag in Japan – that meant detachment of a cruiser. It was time to replace *Nürnburg,* which was stationed on the west coast of Mexico, doing the same job there. *Emden* was due for a partial refit, which could be accomplished in the Tsingtao naval yard, but which would take time. The British cruiser force was coming up to Tsingtao to pay a courtesy call – which meant to take a look. Von Spee was scheduled to make a long-overdue trip to the colonies in the South Seas to check on the efficiency of their defence and remind the natives that German sea power was real.

No matter how von Spee sliced it, his force was going to be much too thin this summer to concentrate anywhere. And there was nothing in the world he could do about it. So the messages went back and forth, and the assignments were made, and the little force of cruisers scurried busily about the oceans. In June, the big cruisers *Scharnhorst* and *Gneisenau* remained in harbour at Tsingtao, along with *Emden*. They would welcome the British and explain the whereabouts of the rest of the force casually, so the foreigners would understand that the little power they saw represented only a summer navy. They would also train their replacements, for each year when the replacement ship came to Tsingtao it was not only an exciting time but a painful one, until the new men grew used to the Orient and to the squadron's ways.

In one sense, service in the Orient was easy, because the back-breaking work such as coaling and scrubbing was done largely by coolie labour. But in another sense, Asian assignment was more difficult, for each sailor, down to the lowest, was expected to be an ambassador of His Majesty, and not all sailors were able to conform to such exalted status.

With the coming of the British cruiser *Minotaur* and the state visit of Vice-Admiral Jerram, the Asiatic commander, the Germans put on the dog as was expected. Governor Meyer-Waldeck brought out the Rhine wine for a huge ball at the palace. Admiral von Spee turned *Scharnhorst* into a floating reception hall for a party almost as grand. The foreign colony came with delight; this kind of entertainment had made Tsingtao famous throughout the Orient as *the* summer spa. And in the romance and the pleasurability of it all the tensions of Europe were forgotten.

Yet they would persist in returning. The merchant captains who called at Tsingtao were a rowdy but bright lot, with a camaraderie among them that cut through national prejudices (except that nearly all of them were loyal reserve officers of their own navies), and they talked with quiet presentiment of a war that seemed a million miles away. One of them, Captain Julius Lauterbach, was so certain that war was coming that summer that he advanced his usual reserve training period so that he would have 'broken in' well before the time came to fight: he left the deck of his merchant ship, the *Staatssekretär Krätke*, and joined the force of *Emden*, just to make ready.

Yet nothing at all had happened.

Two months, said the knowledgable Lauterbach as he quaffed a stein of beer in the *Offizierkasino* ashore. Two months he would give it, and then war!

Lauterbach's source was a Dutch bishop who had just travelled over the Trans-Siberian railroad to return to China after his regular leave at home. The bishop's train coming east had been sidetracked half a dozen times in the European and Ural areas, while troop trains were moved the other way from the east. So what did that mean? The bishop also swore that these troops were being emplanted by the Russians all around the perimeter of the German and Austro-Hungarian empires. The Czar was up to something, said the bishop – and Lauterbach believed him.

But the other officers of the East Asia squadron believed the big fat merchant captain no more than did Admiral Jerram, who laughed aloud when Lauterbach announced his fears of a Russian-German conflict. The world had never been more peaceful, said Jerram with conviction, as he returned from the snipe hunt that afternoon and they settled down in von Spee's quarters for a glass of sherry.

Von Spee could not but catch the absolute sincerity in Jerram's voice, and it would have been nice to believe. But something hung in the air, and von Spee's responsibilities were far too great for him to relax. Berlin was piling up mountains of paper, examining and re-examining the roles of the cruiser force in the world, and particularly the part to be played by Admiral von Spee's squadron in case of hostilities.

Von Spee did not even have time to read all of it, for at the end of the month he had to be off on that projected voyage first to the Marianas, then the Carolines, and Samoa, to inspect those colonies and report to Berlin on the state of their defences.

After that he would pay calls at Fiji, Bougainville, and the Bismarck archipelago, and make his way back in a leisurely fashion to Tsingtao, arriving at the end of September. The arrangements for this trip had been costly to the German government, for there was no natural coal to be found in these islands. A number of colliers had been laid on, some to be sent out from Tsingtao, some to be dispatched from Japan.

So with a flurry of glad music, with flags flying, the two big cruisers left Tsingtao one bright summer day, and left Captain Karl von Müller, commander of the *Emden*, as senior officer in charge of the defence of the colony. Arrangements were made for von Spee to keep in close touch with the base, through the wireless stations at Tsingtao and Yap, and for von Müller to keep the rest of the command informed of activity through the cable to Shanghai. Von Spee was not worried about his communications – new radio stations at Nauru and Apia could keep the squadron informed.

From Tsingtao, von Müller was to relay messages to the elements of the command on the Asiatic coast. These were: *Korvettenkapitän* Luring in the *Jaguar*, who was patrolling along the Yangtse river; *Korvettenkapitän* Thierichens in the *Luchs*, on duty in the port of Shanghai at the moment. Other vessels of the command were flung as far out. But *Korvettenkapitän* von Bodecker in *Tiger* was right there in Tsingtao. So was *Korvettenkapitän* Fritz Sachsse, who had the gunboat *Iltis* in the dry dock at the moment.

Then there were the little *Flusskanonenbooten,* or fast gun-boats. *Tsingtao,* under *Kapitänleutnant* von Moeller, was in the West river, on duty. *Oberleutnant* Dressler had taken *Vaterland* to the Yangtse, and there gone up river to join *Otter* under *Kapitänleutnant* Seuffert. In case of war against Russia, it was quite conceivable that the gunboats on the rivers could be brought back to squadron headquarters and then deployed against the enemy in the north. But in case of war with England, as everyone knew, the chances of these boats ever getting back to Tsingtao were slim.

Oberleutnant Brunner, the commander of the torpedo boat S-90, was away as well. He had just taken his little craft out into the Gulf of Petschili on a training mission.

As the month neared its end, Captain von Müller moved the pins around the map, according to information he received from Berlin, the captains, and from von Spee off on his trip to the south. *Geier,* the ship that had been on the Australian station, was on her way to the Far East, and was expected to put in at Singapore on 25 July. *Cormoran,* under *Korvettenkapitän* Zuckschwerdt, was going into dry dock very shortly in Tsingtao for a refit. The survey ship *Planet* was in the South Seas, taking soundings and gathering information for new charts of the area. There, plus the 4,500 Europeans ashore, including 4,300 Germans, was the European contingent of the command over which the absent von Spee held jurisdiction. This summer, as the rumours and the flood of information from Berlin increased, it seemed a very thin line.

A week after von Spee had left Tsingtao, the tension was very high. So on 29 June, Captain von Müller could be grateful for at least one thing: he had news of the murder of the Archduke Franz Ferdinand at Sarajevo. There, said Lieutenant Lauterbach, late a captain in the merchant service, it was just what the Dutch bishop had been warning against. The heir to the Austro-Hungarian empire shot down on a visit of state. The Russians had been up to something all the while.

The news from the admiralty was not very enlightening at first. All Berlin could say was that the situation was not clear, and that the admiralty would keep von Spee and his command informed. Von Spee, down in the middle of the Carolines, was warned to stick close to Truk or Ponape. Then began a storm of situation reports, as ships at sea, agents in various neutral places, and naval attaches reported on the movement of elements of the European fleets.

Emden and *Tiger* were scheduled for a tour of the Yangtse, but this was stopped and von Müller was ordered to keep both ships in Tsingtao and move the gunboats in the Chinese interior around as necessary.

On 25 July, the authorities in Berlin warned Admiral von Spee that Austro-Hungary had sent an ultimatum to Siberia over the assassination of the archduke, and that matters appeared grim. Next day, von Spee told von Müller in Tsingtao that he was to move his Yangtse river boats, and that the repairs to the *Jaguar*, in Shanghai for partial refit, must either be abandoned or speeded up. So those orders went out along the China station.

Meanwhile the sense of urgency was increased when the Austro-Hungarian cruiser *Kaiserin Elizabeth* pulled into this friendly port to await developments. The Austrian ship was not of much use as a fighting vessel, she was old and slow and outmoded. But her presence reminded everyone in Tsingtao that Austria-Hungary was the immutable ally of the German Imperial government, and that this crisis must be resolved very soon.

Every day brought more bad news. On 27 July the admiralty reported briskly: diplomatic relations between Austro-Hungary and Serbia were broken. Captain von Müller called *Luchs* to come from Shanghai and *S-90* from Chefoo – both to head for the home port of Tsingtao.

It was a worrisome time.

Berlin reported the British cruiser *Newcastle* in Nagasaki, and the French heavy cruiser *Dupleix* in Hakodate. Against such force, Tsingtao at the moment lay virtually undefended.

Then at the end of the month came the terse word: War.

The war at the moment had broken out between Austro-Hungary and Serbia, but Russia would be in momentarily, and then the alliances would begin to feel the strain. Russia and France and Britain were allies, as opposed to Germany and Austria, and Japan had that treaty with the British.

Berlin did not go into details. Tsingtao was still stunned, but did not need details. The course was clear: the station and all the ships must mobilize for war. Berlin made it apparent: she was sending 10,000 tons of coal to the China station immediately for the use of the cruiser squadron.

If possible, all the gunboats should be recalled to Tsingtao, but it was not possible, as von Müller knew, for all of them to get there. They would have to do the best they could. The warnings went out, to the ships of the force and the colliers and other German vessels on the high seas: they must be prepared for war with France, England and Russia. Ships on the high seas, then, should head for the nearest German or neutral port.

All this fearsome responsibility rested on the shoulders of Captain von Müller, in the absence of the admiral. On 30 July the captain called a meeting aboard his ship *Emden* of all commanders in the area, from Governor Meyer-Waldeck down to the captain of *S-90*. They came aboard that morning to discover that *Emden* was in the process of stripping down for action. In the past she had been a comfortable seagoing fortress, with fine wood panelling in the officers' mess and quarters, in the ship's library and the petty officers' mess. Now all that panelling was torn out, to reveal the unlovely and jutting surfaces of weapons and steel plates. Everything flammable was removed and sent ashore to be stored for a less tumultuous hour.

Von Müller assembled his lesser commanders and told them that they must do likewise with all they oversaw. By this time the commanders of three of the gunboats had showed up, along with Brunner of the *S-90* and the governor. Von Müller gave them a briefing on the course of events in the last few days, the situation of the admiralty in Berlin, and the squadron in the South Seas, and told them to make ready. The *Cormoran* he found was in immediate need of repairs. So orders were issued and that very afternoon she was moved into dry dock.

The collier *Elsbeth* was loading for Ponape, where she was to make contact with the cruiser squadron. The captain was told to speed it up and get going: war with Russia was expected momentarily.

The gunboat captains were told what would be expected of them: they would either go out to sea as escorts for various colliers and merchant cruisers that would be armed at Tsingtao, or they would be left for the defence of the port. The Yangtse gunboats were on their way, the captain announced, but it would take a few days for them to arrive.

CHAPTER FIVE

The War Begins

With the orders from Tsingtao, the gunboat *Jaguar* set forth from Shanghai. She was followed in short order by *Tsingtao* which headed north from Canton, and *Otter*, which was working round Hankow. The survey ship *Planet* was told to head into Rabaul and report to Admiral von Spee for orders; she was too far away to come home even if she could have been of any conceivable use in a crisis.

On 31 July, a white and nervous Captain von Müller decided that he would take the cruiser *Emden* out to sea. The authorities in Berlin indicated hourly that war was coming closer, and was almost inevitable. What if a British cruiser force appeared outside Tsingtao to attack? *Emden* could never get out, although if she was outside she could expect to evade and outrun the heavier ships. The decision was a weighty one, and von Müller conferred with Captain Meyer-Waldeck, for after all von Müller represented the cruiser squadron, and one of its responsibilities was the protection of the harbour of Tsingtao.

Meyer-Waldeck, being a naval captain, quite understood von Müller's reasoning and encouraged him in his desire to get to sea in case action might begin in the next few hours. So the dummy torpedo warheads were unloaded from *Emden*, all combustibles were brought ashore, the hospital was raided for the walking sick who could return to duty, and last minute coal and stores were put aboard the light cruiser. She was preparing, pell-mell, for sea.

From the south came the word that von Spee was also preparing, as best he could, the various colonial forces for their own defence. Virtually no preparation was possible – the colonies had never been established as military outposts, and the only

B

reason Tsingtao was fortified round the land perimeter was to protect the city from Chinese bandits and warlords, that idea being gained from the troubles of the Boxer days.

Of course there were all kinds of intelligence reports and rumours about the potential enemy. Most important, to von Müller, was the report on 31 July that the big British cruiser force had in fact left Weihaiwei and was now at sea.

So von Müller moved. He ordered steam up, and he ordered the collier *Elsbeth* to be ready to move, for he would escort her outside the harbour and see her on her way south towards the squadron, before he did anything else.

At 1900 hours, just as dark was falling over the harbour, *Emden* and *Elsbeth* headed out. The crew was summoned at the moment of sailing and told for the first time that war was very near, and that they would now go on a war watch basis, which meant four hours on duty and eight off instead of the easy four hours on duty in every twenty-four that marked the peacetime navy.

Outside the point, suddenly the drums beat and the bugles blew. It was the first time since the war scare began.

'Action stations' came the order. The watertight doors were clanged and locked, the lights doused, and men went to their battle stations, at guns, searchlights, torpedo tubes, and in the engine rooms.

But it was a false alarm, the glimmer of light on a wave top, and there was nothing on the sea to disturb them. After two hours the ship settled down, the blowers were turned back on, the portholes opened, and life assumed some semblance of normality.

That night *Emden* steamed southeast towards the mid-Pacific colonies, until 2300, when she turned away with a salute to the *Elsbeth*. The collier was now well out to sea, off the normal shipping lanes, and she could be expected to have a very good chance of reaching her destination no matter what luck befell the politicians in Europe.

Captain von Müller now laid his course for Quelpart island, just off the shipping lanes to the north. Here he might hope to catch an enemy steamer – once he knew who the enemy was going to be. For this was the trade route to Korea, to northern Japan, and to the Russian port of Vladivostok.

Von Müller was now alone, and out of sight of land, and his link with official reality was the wireless that brought him a constant stream of messages from the big station atop the mountain at Tsingtao. He steamed for his destination, and he waited. The night of 31 July passed very slowly.

Back in Tsingtao, Captain Meyer-Waldeck now had the awesome responsibility of reading all the messages, day and night, and making the decisions as to what was to be sent on to Yap and the southern stations, and what steps were to be taken for the defence of Kiaochow colony. There was a plan, of course, and this *Mobilmachung* was set to go into effect on orders from Berlin. But preliminary action was in order, and Meyer-Waldeck had to manage it. Supplies were unpacked from godowns around the city and brought to garrison headquarters. Unnecessary, if useful, work was stopped on painting and repair projects, and the workmen and coolies were put to strengthening the defences of the garrison.

The naval troops were not exactly lax in their drill and readiness, but neither were they keyed up for action. Meyer-Waldeck sought to remedy this state of affairs; close-order drill was ordered daily, and every man's equipment was inspected and needs met as far as possible from the supply godowns.

Leutnant Gunther Pluschow, the aviator, was sunk in despair at this moment, for like the other officers he sensed the worry of his superiors, and had for days, without a situation briefing being held. The mobilization of *Emden,* although carried out as a drill until she got to sea, had fooled no one ashore. Pluschow was upset at this moment because his airplane was not performing as he had hoped.

That was putting it nicely. The airplane had arrived along with the balloons and the small detachment of men from Germany, and Pluschow had begun his training in July. Captain Meyer-Waldeck was not quite certain of the value of the airplane to his command, and he certainly was not going to build a special aerodrome for one plane. Berlin would never countenance that action. So he had assigned Pluschow the interior of the racecourse for his field.

At first look, the racecourse appeared to make a fine airfield. It was flat. But on second look, it was tiny – just 200 yards wide and only 600 yards long. On three sides it was bounded by hills full of beckoning pine trees. On the ocean side another hill rose up just beyond the end of the runway, and then dropped off into the sea. The whole effect was rather more alpine than less, from Pluschow's point of view.

Then there was the wind. The engineer who had designed the racecourse was immensely proud of his location and planning, for no matter how hot the day in Tsingtao or in the hills around, the bowl effect of the mountains on three sides, and the sea beyond with its hill between, gave a breeze to the racecourse. The breeze was inconstant, it came from this side and then from that and it gusted and whirled and sometimes blew up whirlwinds of dust. But that was a small price to pay for the cooling effect of the breezes on a hot midsummer's day.

When the aircraft arrived, of course it was crated up. Coolies had loaded it off the ship, and brought it to the aerodrome, where Pluschow was occupying himself by teaching his new detachment of balloonists how to put up the two big sausage-shaped barrage balloons with their observer's baskets. The aerodrome with its command of the bay beyond was an excellent spotting point for the artillery.

The plane was a low-winged monoplane, with oddly shaped 'dove-type' wings, that had scalloping on the trailing edge, on the theory that birds' wings were scalloped and this must have something to do with the stability of birds in flight. It was a two-

place plane with a 100 horsepower Mercedes engine, driving a
two-bladed wooden propeller.

By the time of Sarajevo, Pluschow had his plane put together
and was ready to fly. He was somewhat apprehensive about the
shortness of the 'runway' and the gusty air currents that he
must face on take-off and landing, but he took off one bright
sunny day, flew round the bay and landed safely. It was a new
experience for the people of Tsingtao. The Chinese had never
seen an airplane before; the monster kite made a dreadful racket
but it also sped along. Many of the Europeans had never seen a
plane in flight before, either, for aviation was very young in this
summer of 1914, and had been confined to a handful of enthu-
siasts in many parts of Germany.

The first flight was a success – qualified only by Captain
Meyer-Waldeck's obvious lack of enthusiasm. The governor was
jubilant over the coming of Pluschow and the barrage balloons.
These were something a man could understand, and an aspect
of harbour defence that had been sorely overlooked in previous
planning. High though the hills of Tsingtao might be, the range
of naval guns was growing ever longer, and a bombarding force
could sit off the harbour and train in on the ships and fortifications, yet be difficult to place from shore. But with these
balloons operating from the mountains, the work of the artillery
spotters was much lessened and made more accurate.

But the airplane, that toy of Berlin, well, Meyer-Waldeck would
wait and see how long it lasted and what it accomplished. At the
moment he hoped his new balloon officer and the son of an old
friend would not break his neck with the flying machine.

On his first flight of about twenty minutes, Pluschow was so
busy familiarizing himself with the plane that he did little else.
He made a safe but bumpy landing. On his second flight he began
to look round a bit, and tested the air currents in the vicinity of
the field. They were as treacherous as he had feared. On his
third flight he skimmed round the bay, rose and dived, and
practised a few aerobatics. Landing was a problem, the field

was 400 yards shorter than he would have liked, but he was a skilful pilot, and he managed.

The fourth flight was again made on one of those bright almost windless days of Shantung summer – 31 July, the very day that Captain von Müller was making ready to head out to sea. And everyone at the aerodrome swore that there was no wind. Yet, as *Leutnant* Pluschow came in for landing, one of the famous racecourse breezes sprang up out of nowhere, swirled across the field, and caught him just as he cut the power of the Taube and the wheels were ready to touch down. The gust grabbed the bird-style tail of the plane with its tall stabilizer elevator and long tail skid. The tail went up, and the nose went down. The wooden propeller hit the ground and turned and hit the ground again, and broke into a dozen pieces. The wing turned and scraped as the fuselage slid along the ground, the framework snapped and the doped fabric tore and rolled off the splinters.

In a minute it was all over. The plane skidded to a stop. *Leutnant* Pluschow shakily pulled himself from the rear cockpit. The enlisted men and the coolies came running on to the field to see if he was killed, and he waved airily at them to show that he was all right. But the plane, as he turned to look at it, was a dreadful mess. The wings were shattered and the undercarriage smashed. The fuselage was bent and broken. The propeller was in pieces.

Yet in these early days of flying, the airplane was not so complicated an instrument as it might appear. Pluschow was really concerned that day about the state of the engine. He looked it over carefully, and it seemed almost undamaged. The propeller had taken the brunt of the crash, along with the wing, and the engine could be fixed with a wrench and a hammer. And in the godown assigned to the aviation section were crates and crates of spare wing parts, already mounted with doped fabric, and more propellers.

Or so he thought.

When *Leutnant* Pluschow ordered up the first wing crate he

opened it with pleasure, and then with dismay as he saw before him a twisted mass of rotting fabric and wooden sections in which the glue had come unstuck. Whoever had packed up these parts had made no allowance for changes in humidity and temperature and these effects on doped fabric. The parts were completely unusable. Each crate yielded the same findings, until the cases were all torn apart. And the propellers: one after another was brought out for Pluschow's examination, and every one was discarded. All had warped and the glue had come unstuck.

Pluschow went down to headquarters and demanded an interview with Captain Meyer-Waldeck. Parts must be ordered up immediately from Berlin, he said. The plane would not fly.

Meyer-Waldeck was really too busy to listen to his young lieutenant. The flow of messages from Berlin was growing ever more urgent; it was obviously just a matter of hours until war with Russia began. Absently the captain told the lieutenant to order up what he needed by wireless. With the sinking feeling that the material would never arrive in time, *Leutnant* Pluschow listed all his needs, including another airplane, and sent off the message to Berlin. Then he went back to the airfield to consult with his petty officer, and the Chinese coolies. What a mess he was in, and what a hard way to struggle against an insane bureaucracy that did not know how to package up an airplane.

The petty officer and the German enlisted men could offer Pluschow little but sympathy, but the Chinese looked over the broken plane, and one of them suggested that this was not so much different from the kites they had been making for thousands of years. If the foreigners wished, they would consult with the expert kitemakers, and see if something could not be done to make the bird-machine fly again.

There – at least Pluschow had hope. The alternative was to do nothing but play with barrage balloons. It was necessary that the training of the balloonists continue, but this pro-gramme could be handled very well by the petty officer with a little supervision. *Leutnant* Pluschow sent the Chinese back to the Chinese city to consult with his experts, and began picking up the pieces of the broken Taube.

Down at the grey stone headquarters, Governor Meyer-Waldeck sensed that the crisis was near. It came next day, from Berlin: *'Am 1 August ist die Mobilmachung von Heer und Marine befohlen. . . .'*

Mobilization. . . .

The Operation Plan was in effect, and Governor Meyer-Waldeck moved to the safe and brought it forth in the absence of any superior officer.

This meant war.

CHAPTER SIX

Operations

The mobilization of German forces in the Far East was complicated immensely by that unfortunate trip scheduled by Admiral
von Spee to the South Seas in that fateful summer of 1914.
Captain and Governor Meyer-Waldeck had never been faced
with the idea that he would have to supervise the mobilization
of much of the force himself, so it took him a good bit of time
to read up on his assignment that day and night. The forces
might not be large, but they were so far flung that the job was
complicated.

Governor Meyer-Waldeck proclaimed a state of military emergency in the colony, which meant martial law. He sent warnings
around to all the hotels on the beach, and posted notices in
every public place. Then he began the specific welding together
of the colony's defence.

All coolies were impressed for military service at forty cents
a day. Some managed to escape the city and its environs before
the order was promulgated, with that alert ear to the bamboo
telegraph that all shared. They left the colony fearfully short
of impressed labour.

Passage on the railway was now restricted to those with
government permits. That stopped the coolies from escaping,
but also impressed the foreigners with the nearness of war.

Postal service to 'enemies' was cut off, and parcels were
accepted only for Germany, Austria, China, Japan, and the
United States.

Orders were made ready (they would not be issued for a
few days) for all Russians to leave the colony. Germans were
recalled from Harbin and other Manchurian towns, and from

B*

the Shantung rail zone and Kiaochow bay, and the machinery was set in motion to mine the approaches to the harbour.

Navigation lights and lighthouses were extinguished. Plans were made for the absolute blackout of the city. Foreigners were urged to leave the city and go to places where their own nationals would be able to protect them. The train service was increased to get the foreigners out of town.

The commander of Tsingtao was ordered to detain all vessels of enemy nations – once the enemy was established – and to warn all neutrals that they must observe strictly the conditions of neutrality. Also, so neutral ships would not become a burden on the economy of the colony, they were sharply restricted in their length of stay and the amount of coal they might take on at the port. In order to accomplish this, Captain Meyer-Waldeck had to set up a new organization.

Tsingtao, under the admiralty plan, was also designated as an assembly point for naval colliers. Over the past few years the admiralty had very carefully maintained an extremely large fleet of coal ships in the Pacific and the Orient, in the eventuality of a war. At this moment these ships were scattered around the whole of the Orient and Pacific on various errands. They supplied the other German colonies in the Pacific, and they drew their coal here in Shantung province and sometimes from Darien and other coal ports of the Orient. Tsingtao was to be the assembly point for these ships, which would then continue to supply the German positions, and particularly the cruiser squadron.

The German position at Tsingtao was also important as one of two major information stations in the Pacific, the less important being on the island of Yap. All the information that Berlin wanted to reach German nationals and German colonies and German ships at sea would pass through Tsingtao, and be relayed on to the less powerful receivers and transmitters around the Pacific.

Tsingtao was also to be the assembly point of the gunboat fleet stationed in East Asia. *Iltis, Jaguar, Luchs,* and *Tiger* would all come back to roost and then would be used as the admiralty directed, in the best interest of the German war effort. At this late date it had to be assumed that the fast gunboats in the Yangtse and the south would be unable to disengage from the enemy. But the crews were to try to make their way back to Tsingtao, where they would be assigned by Admiral von Spee or the commander of the garrison to auxiliary cruisers.

The auxiliary cruiser was a very important element in the German war plan. For months Berlin had been sending along extra ammunition, extra guns, uniforms and all the supplies that would be needed to turn innocent merchantmen into fast arms of the German navy. The idea was that a big passenger ship or a fast cargo ship of modern design could be armed with one or more large guns. Such would be enough to capture any ordinary merchantman, and by making use of these ships the Germans would be able to overcome their numerical deficiency in actual warships in the far regions of the world. Further, the real fighting ships of the East Asia cruiser squadron, and of other areas, would be freed then for far more important tasks than the war of attrition that was to starve out England, if she got into the war. In time of war any ship of any German line was automatically a servant of the crown, and could be commandeered to become a *Hilfskreuzer*. Since every man jack of the German merchant marine was also automatically a member of the naval reserve, there would be no trouble about manning the ships. There were no conscientious objectors in the German marine.

Some parts of the operation plan, of course, did not directly affect Tsingtao, for the admiral's area of responsibility was the whole Pacific, but Captain Meyer-Waldeck skimmed those, and concentrated his attention on the matters that concerned him.

In June, before he sailed away for the South Seas, Admiral von Spee had left certain other instructions for Captain von Müller as the senior officer on the station. Von Müller was to call in all coal ships on the day of mobilization, and to make sure that several got off to the south to aid the cruiser squadron if anything happened while von Spee was away.

Then came the message from Berlin that everyone was waiting for. *Emden* had been gone two days, when von Müller's hunch was verified: it was war with Russia. When the news came to the light cruiser, she was almost directly on the steamer route that ran between Weihaiwei and Hong Kong. It was 2 August, a Sunday, and von Müller had just finished church services when the word was passed from the wireless room.

At that moment, Admiral Jerram of the British fleet was already in operation, just as much as von Müller. Jerram had gone to Weihaiwei in July and on 28 July his cruiser force was lying in that safe haven to the north of Tsingtao. As the German air waves were crackling with messages about the political situation, so were the British, and there were just as many kinky details to be ironed out in the British plan as there were in the German. Admiral Jerram was in his flagship, *Minotaur*. With him were the cruisers *Hampshire* and *Yarmouth*, the gunboat *Thistle*, and the destroyers *Welland*, *Ribble*, *Usk*, *Colne*, and *Kennet*. They had spent much of the summer doing the same thing that Admiral von Spee was doing in the South Pacific – showing the flag. At Weihaiwei they were coaling at leisure, taking a rest, and putting in supplies when the warning telegram arrived on 28 July.

Jerram had the same complications in his own life that von Spee was suffering. His light cruiser *Newcastle* was over in Japan, making a courtesy call at Nagasaki. Three British gunboats were at Shanghai, and six more were on the Yangtse – which was one of the major reasons Admiral von Spee and Berlin could agree it was most unlikely that the German craft in waters south of Tsingtao would be able to join and be usable by the squadron.

Down in Hong Kong, the battleship *Triumph* was in dry dock, demobbed for the moment. The sloop of war *Clio* was refitting. There were three more destroyers in Hong Kong, *Jed*, *Chalmer*, and *Fame*, and four more gunboats, three Class C submarines, and four torpedo boats. Obviously this force was superior in every way to that of von Spee, who knew it well. Obviously the British

were the problem in East Asian waters, if war came with England.
Jerram sat in Weihaiwei, waiting as he was told to do for
further orders. 29 July brought only the crackling of the wireless
and no satisfaction whatever. Next day, however, he received
the formal Warning Telegram which put him on Warning
Orders, and that meant action. The first thing Jerram did was
mobilize *Triumph* in dry dock, and order the Yangtse gunboats on the lower end of the stream to lay up and the crews to
proceed to man the battleship.

At the moment of the warning, Jerram's information concerning
the whereabouts of his potential enemy was as spotty as von
Spee's was about the English. The word in the south Pacific was
that the *Australia* and several other heavy ships were out searching
for the East Asia squadron in China waters. That was nonsense.
The British did not really know where von Spee was. They did
know, from excellent intelligence, precisely what was in Tsingtao
harbour – except that Jerram's information was a bit old for, by
the time he received it, von Müller had already sailed in his
nervousness to get into action.

The Warning Telegram put Admiral Jerram in more control
of his fate than he had enjoyed before. He could, within limits,
decide where to concentrate next, and he decided to put his
squadron outside Tsingtao and wait for the German capital
ships *Scharnhorst* and *Gneisenau* to head back. These were the
dangers as the British saw them – the light cruisers, the gunboats
and torpedo boats did not offer any particular threat, given the
strength of the British defences of the Asian colonies.

But London had other plans. Winston Churchill, the First
Lord of the Admiralty, believed that Jerram should move
swiftly down to Hong Kong to supervise the readying of *Triumph*
and the organization of his force. Three Canadian Pacific liners
were in Hong Kong and one P & O liner was also there. All
four could be turned into auxiliary cruisers, and Churchill and
the others in London wanted to be certain that Jerram supervised the job personally. As far as London knew there was

nothing in Tsingtao worth worrying about. There were much larger fish to fry. London was aware of the German plan to arm its passenger vessels and fast freighters, and London was frankly very much worried over the prospects. Thus *Empress of Asia, Empress of Japan, Empress of Russia,* and *Himalaya* were to be given guns and naval crews and turned into parts of His Majesty's naval force, with the very specific duty of protecting merchantmen and ferreting out and fighting the German fleet of auxiliary cruisers that was expected to be unleashed in the next few days.

So with considerable reluctance, Admiral Jerram gave up his plan to lie off Tsingtao, and turned southward. So close was the British squadron to *Emden* at that moment that as night fell and the little cruiser moved onwards, her watch reported *Kiel-wasser.* Sure enough, when the captain came to the bridge there it was – the lingering wake that churned up the phosphorescence of these seas and left a track for hours after a ship had passed.

Of course had they met at that moment or that day, nothing would have happened. Britain and Germany were still officially at peace, although not a man among the crews of the ships doubted what was to come. But if they had met, then the British would have trailed *Emden* thereafter, and her forthcoming adventures would never have occurred as they did.

For *Emden* steamed north, searching for a Russian ship, and off the Korean coast she found one – the Russian mail steamer *Rjasan,* which plied between Vladivostok and Shanghai on a regular run. She was a vessel of 3,500 tons, Lloyd's registry showed, and Lieutenant Lauterbach, the old merchant skipper, had been aboard her many times and knew she was modern and carried a wireless.

The wireless did not save her this day. A shot went across the Russian's bow, and a boarding party was sent to take her. In a few hours the prize crew was bringing the first trophy of the war back to Tsingtao. Had Jerram been on station as he wished, he still could have done nothing at the moment but watch as

Emden paraded her prize. But neither of them would ever have got out of Tsingtao harbour again.

On the way back to Tsingtao, von Müller learned from the prize crew of the Russian ship that the Russians had already told the world about the capture before they were taken. That wireless had proved as great a problem as Captain von Müller had feared. So with unusual caution, the captain of the *Emden* moved towards his home port. On the afternoon of 5 August he learned that he was at war with France and with England too, and that if enemy vessels were around he might have to fight his way.

Captain von Müller assumed that the British would be standing off Tsingtao waiting for him, and he acted accordingly. On the way he spotted a number of Japanese vessels, who dipped their flags courteously for they were not at war, and he thought he saw the mastheads of the French cruisers *Montcalm* and *Dupleix*, and made every effort to avoid them. Then he reached the waters off Tsingtao and waited carefully for darkness to make his approach. But all was well. At 0300 on the morning of 6 August, Captain von Müller took his ship in past the light and the rocks off the harbour, and was home safely. As he reached the harbour he waited for a pilot, because in his absence Captain Meyer-Waldeck had supervised the laying of a mine field. Outside the field, the steamer CS *Leiss* joined them for the ingress – she had been waiting for several hours for passage in. As they came around the corner and saw the city laid out before them, they also saw that it was totally dark. Captain Meyer-Waldeck had accomplished another part of his job – the blackout of the European and Chinese cities was complete. Tsingtao knew that it was at war.

CHAPTER SEVEN

The Lonely Command

On the voyage into harbour, *Emden* saw precautions that had never been there before. Near the island of Matau, the cruiser signalled with a lamp to show that she was on her way in, and in these last minutes of darkness before the dawn the signal was answered. Then came the reverberation of a warning shot across the water, for the harbour command at Tsingtao was alerting the defence force that a ship was coming in. No chances were being taken here.

Up came the gunboat *Jaguar* to look over the *Emden*. Not that anyone doubted it was she, but *Jaguar*'s job was to do just this, and see that no enemy submarines or other vessels could be tailing along behind in the darkness.

It was 0600 hours when *Emden* pulled in at the familiar naval basin and anchored, and already along the quay the people were beginning to assemble. For the bamboo telegraph had told Tsingtao much about what had happened on the high seas in the past week. *Emden* had engaged in a mighty battle with the Russian cruiser *Askold*, and had beaten her and taken the *Rjasan* as a prize – that was the bamboo telegraph story. It had the prize part right, but the story of the *Askold* was the purest of invention. Nonetheless, the people of Tsingtao flocked to the harbour to see the heroic wounded (of which there were none) and to wait for the coming of *Rjasan* which was standing outside the mine field waiting for an escort.

Finally she came and, as she eased up to the steamship dock, German war-flag flying, the cheers were tremendous, the bandsmen broke out their music and Tsingtao gave itself over to an emotional celebration. The war was on, the war was being fought by the heroic German sailors, the war was being won.

Captain von Müller had very little time to enjoy the festivities. He sent a brisk note to the surgeon commanding the naval hospital across the mountain: no he would not need the beds reserved for the victims of the fight with *Askold* because there had been no fight. He cast his eye across the celebration – and then he brought *Emden* into the coaling dock and began filling the cruiser with hard black coal.

Theoretically von Müller was still in charge at Tsingtao. In fact, he already had his sailing orders: he was to leave almost immediately for Pagan, where he would meet with the other ships of the East Asia squadron, and then Admiral Graf von Spee would decide what disposition he was going to make of his force, in view of the tactical situation he faced. Von Müller knew what he wanted to do – go raiding enemy commerce in the Indian Ocean – but for that venture he must have the permission of his commander.

So, his head full of plans and worries about his ship and her war readiness, Captain von Müller had little time or attention to devote to the defences of Tsingtao. He called a meeting of the commanders and listened to the problems as they were outlined by Captain Meyer-Waldeck. Von Müller's major contribution was to suggest the conversion of *Rjasan*, the fine new Russian mail steamer, to an auxiliary cruiser which would go out and raid enemy commerce. That plan meant the end of the old gunboat *Cormoran*, and even the end of the ship's name, for the *Rjasan* would assume it. Von Müller's other bit of advice, not very happy for the Austrian captain of *Kaiserin Elizabeth*, was that she be kept in harbour at all costs, because outside she was no more than a sitting duck for the first enemy destroyer that might come by.

The meeting was held at the governor's palace, where von Müller repaired himself to give official word of his coming departure and the passing of command of Tsingtao to the governor. It was not a very generous gift, and von Müller knew it, for since the whole defence plan of Tsingtao had been built about the existence of the cruiser squadron in the harbour or just outside, and now the squadron was deserting the colony, he was leaving it to the inadequate force of gunboats and the handful of soldiers and sailors in uniform that Meyer-Waldeck could muster.

6 August, the day after the declaration of war against France and England, was one of feverish activity in the port. The boats of *Emden* were scurrying about begging all the stores that Captain von Müller needed. On the piers, anti-aircraft guns were mounted for harbour defence. On the edge of the harbour, on the cape, more anti-aircraft guns were mounted, until the harbour was ringed with pom-poms and bigger guns.

Captain Meyer-Waldeck sat at his big desk in the palace and read the cables that came rushing in like gulls to a feeding ground. He had all the news and rumours of the enemy activity in his area and throughout Asia. He had the news that the German army was marching. He had word that the Japanese were neutral, although the naval attaché at Shanghai did not believe Japan would be neutral long. Already the Japanese consul in Hong Kong was sending messages that Germans on Formosa would be interned, and that certainly did not sound very neutral. And from Swatow, Hong Kong and Shanghai came report after report that the Japanese had already made up their minds to march against the Germans – and their destination would be Tsingtao, the colony the Japanese wanted for their own purposes.

Meyer-Waldeck knew as much about the Graf von Spee's plans as did Captain von Müller, for the squadron commander that day extinguished all hope that he would return to fight his war in East Asian waters. He announced to Tsingtao that he would go either into the Indian Ocean to destroy commerce and seek battle with Jerram's force, or he would move into the broad Pacific, round Cape Horn, re-fuel in Chile, and then head across the Atlantic to join the High Seas fleet and smash the British in their home waters.

From Berlin came another view, offered by Admiral von Spee's immediate superior, Captain Fielitz, the chief of staff of the cruiser squadron command. Fielitz did not outrank von Spee, but being at home he had tremendous influence. He thought the cruiser squadron ought definitely to go into the Indian Ocean and conduct war against the merchant ships to prevent British expansion, although he listed all the dangers – which meant the British capital ships in the area.

As for von Spee, he was a busy man, but he took time that day to comfort Meyer-Waldeck as best he could. 'I have just learned of the Japanese statement of neutrality,' he said. 'I am confident that the British command in Asia will not attack.'

But if that telegram was supposed to allay Meyer-Waldeck's fears, it did not. The Chinese who did not want to live under Japanese domination were already talking about moving inland. The bamboo telegraph was stirring with its reports of Japanese troop movement headed toward Tsingtao.

Next day, Meyer-Waldeck's anxieties were increased when *Korvettenkapitän* von Knorr, the naval attaché in Tokyo, warned that he had word from the German consul in Mukden that the Japanese Manchurian army was making ready to march on Tsingtao.

A number of German passenger ships and freighters had come into Tsingtao harbour in the past few days since the warning telegrams went out to all on the high seas who could receive them. One of these vessels brought a new aircraft and pilot. The aircraft was another Taube, which had already had a long life and had been changed in design. It had begun as an army plane with a 75 horsepower engine and floats. That was back in 1912. Then it was taken back to the factory in Danzig and worked over because it never did fly very well. It was taken to the Rumpler factory and worked over again, and the 75 horsepower engine was removed and a 100 horsepower engine put in. So the float plane for the army was converted into a wheeled plane for the navy in true bureaucratic confusion. And to it was assigned *Leutnant* Mullerskowsky, a bright young flier who had recently graduated from pilot school.

With Pluschow's plane laid up, Mullerskowsky then became the air force of the Germans at Tsingtao, and he started flight preparations that very day, bringing the plane up from the harbour to the tenuous airfield at the racecourse. Pluschow swallowed the lump in his throat and gave all assistance to the new man.

Concerned as he was with the 500 tons of coal he must ship and the other supplies of fresh water and food and ammunition to be taken on, Captain von Müller took time to work with two of the steamers in the harbour. *Prinz Eitel Friedrich,* a 9,000 ton passenger liner, was to be converted to a *Hilfskreuzer.* The guns were installed, the civilian captain was replaced by *Korvettenkapitän* Thierichens, of the gunboat *Luchs,* and she was quickly made ready for sea, for she would go out with *Emden.* The collier *Markomannia* was also jammed to the top with coal, and ordered to go along with *Emden* towards the South Seas.

By rail and junk and sampan, the Chinese began to desert the city. Some had already gone out by ship to seek refuge in British colonies, where they would be safe from the Japanese. But the poor and those who worked directly for the Germans remained to do their duty and await events.

Captain Meyer-Waldeck now devoted nearly all his time to the city's defences. The harbour was officially closed to all foreign shipping, even neutral. The *Kaiserin Elizabeth* was going to be scuttled at the harbour mouth, to prevent the big capital ships of the British navy or the Japanese, for that matter, from coming in. Captain Meyer-Waldeck was becoming ever more apprehensive of a Japanese attack in spite of the messages he was receiving that showed no action. The rumours were there, underlying the surface, and the rumours meant more to him than any official reports or protestations. The colliers began loading the brave old Austrian warship with rocks, for her final resting place. It would be a terrible job to clean up later, the rock-bound ship would be hard to move or destroy, but at the moment she would provide a helpful concomitant to the harbour defences.

The gunboats were in harbour, and Captain Meyer-Waldeck had to worry about what would be done with them. They could not stand up to a destroyer or even a modern torpedo boat in battle. *Iltis, Jaguar* and *Tiger* were most valuable at the moment for their crews and armament. Captain Meyer-Waldeck was considering scuttling them also.

All day long on this 7 August the sailors of the three ships that would soon be leaving did their work in the blazing sun. *Prinz Eitel Friedrich*'s white hull and upper works were white no more. She was painted over drab, to give her a much less striking appearance, and then given the marks of a British P & O liner. Whether or not she would fool anyone with her distinctive lines remained to be seen, but the attempt was made.

Markomannia was also painted, given a blue funnel in the hope that she would be mistaken on the high seas for a Blue Funnel liner under the English flag. For the Germans knew their enemy and they knew whom they might best impersonate at sea. Britannia ruled the waves, much as the Kaiser's subjects hated to admit it. They might challenge her as they were bound to do, but they also recognized that their best chance of escaping detection was to pretend to be British.

Elsewhere in the harbour other colliers were getting ready to go out, too, for Admiral von Spee had now plotted his cruisers' future course, and he had ordered up 5,000 tons of coal for Pagan, 5,000 tons for point A (which was kept secret from all except those who needed to know) and 5,000 tons for point B. *Elsbeth* had already gone and should be well on her way with her 1,800 tons of good coal.

By day's end the first officer of *Emden* could announce from the depths of his exhaustion that the coaling of the ship was finished. The captains of the two converted ships announced that their painting was done and they were as ready as they could be for their new tasks. *Prinz Eitel Friedrich* hardly resembled the vessel that had left Shanghai just five days earlier. Captain Thierichens, late commander of the *Luchs*, had under him the crews of that vessel and *Tiger*, plus others from the merchant ship who had been brought into regular naval status.

Special attention was paid to the radio. Amid traffic between British ships and stations was some in English between British ships and Japanese vessels. From the south came information that the British auxiliary cruiser *Empress of Japan* might be near Tsingtao, so that night as *Emden* sailed, she escorted the two converted merchantmen out of the harbour. Behind them came *S-90* to guard the minefield as they left. And then, after all this spate of activity, the harbour at Tsingtao was suddenly quiet, and the light cruiser, the last of the cruiser squadron, had gone away. It was a very eerie feeling to be alone.

CHAPTER EIGHT

Decision in Tokyo

In the last week, Tsingtao had sent forth five big colliers laden with coal for the cruiser squadron but four more big ships still remained in the harbour, drawing coal and making ready for their voyages to the South Seas. They now had the full attention of the coolies at the coaling wharf, and they came in to load, one by one.

First to load was the OJD *Ahlers*, the last of the colliers to be dispatched to *Sammelplatz B*, the second rendezvous point where the cruiser squadron would coal. The other ships would have to head out for targets of opportunity, or seek neutral havens later.

Captain Meyer-Waldeck was becoming more and more convinced of one thing as the days went on: Japanese ports would not be numbered among the neutral. From Mukden, Tokyo, and the south China cities before German activity closed down, he had the same report time and again: Japan was getting ready to march against Tsingtao. Only the official announcements failed to confirm the activity.

One source of information was Shanghai, which maintained its character as an international city even in these trying days. There were many Germans in Shanghai during July and August, and they managed to acquire information that was moved along the radio circuits to Tsingtao and Berlin.

On 25 July, *Korvettenkapitän* Luring in *Jaguar*, with the personnel of the gunboat *Vaterland*, arrived in Shanghai, hoping to get to Tsingtao from there so they could make themselves useful. They were annoyed, as were all Germans, by the decided lack of neutrality of the Chinese. The British showed their war

flags openly in Chinese waters, but the Chinese naval vessels in
the harbour at Shanghai kept their searchlights trained on the
German vessels in harbour all night long – as though the Germans
could not be trusted while the British could.

But there was no time for political animosity; there was too
much to be done. The merchant ships in Shanghai harbour began
sailing from the port, carrying coal destined for Tsingtao and
Admiral von Spee, and carrying German nationals to places
where they could fight for their country.

It was the same in Tokyo. During the first week of August
1914, Japan was ablaze with rumour. Most foreigners were
concentrated in the big cities, and they rushed to the clubs and
to their consulates to see what they must do. All reservists,
French, German, British and Russian, were immediately called
to the colours, and that meant going home for most of them.
So they packed up, and went down to the ports. What a sight
it was in Yokohama and Kobe that week. For Germans, French
and British were all getting on the same two ships in the harbours,
going home to Europe together so they could fight one another.
On the dock the crowds of Japanese friends, the men in their
western suits and the girls in their kimonos and parasols,
crowded and laughed and cried to see their western friends
going away. And the Europeans, queuing up in lines, looked
across at the enemy lines oddly, even as they waved to their
Japanese friends.

What a change! The war in Europe had seemed very far
away and unreal until 4 August. That was the day the newspapers of Tokyo and Yokohama were filled with the story of
the capture of the *Rjasan* by Captain von Müller in the *Emden*.
All Europeans in Tokyo knew the *Rjasan* and Captain Austin,
her English master, and suddenly to learn that she was taken as a
prize of war, after having been shot at ten times to stop her;
that brought the war home to the Pacific in a hurry.

In the beginning, most foreigners in Tokyo had not known
quite how to act to one another. Old friendships were strained

but they persisted, and the British naval attaché, seeing his German opposite number on the street, would tip his civilian hat and smile wryly. But not after *Rjasan*. That was the turning point, the tinder that flared and made men look upon others as enemies because they came from a different place. There were no more British guests in the German club.

Asahi Shimbun and *Mainichi* both gave huge play to the capture of the Russian mail steamer, and next day all over Japan newspapermen and businessmen began speculating on the effect this threat to Japanese sovereignty would have on world affairs. For to the Japanese Korea was an essential part of empire, captured and made a colony. And the report from ships which had been in contact with *Rjasan* as she fled and radioed for help added fuel to the fire. Captain Austin had been furious with the capture, and claimed that he was within the protection of Korean territorial waters. Not so, declared the Germans. True, they were in Tsushima strait, between Japan and Korea, and the mail ship was heading in toward Tsushima island and protection, but Captain von Müller said flatly that the capture was made in international waters at 35° 5' North longitude, and 19° 39' East latitude.

All the Japanese knew was that *Rjasan* had sailed from Nagasaki, bound for Vladivostok, and she had been taken, with Japanese and Russians, and Japanese mail, aboard. They were furious and upset about it. The capture was an insult to Japan and a threat to the sovereignty of the emperor over Japanese waters.

Officially, Japan's position was still unknown, for it had never been the habit of the Japanese government to inform press or citizens of its projected actions. But the Japanese government was moving along paths of its own, following a plan established many years earlier.

There were no political parties in Japan, just two clans, one of which controlled the navy, while the other controlled the army, and in the war to come there was no ground for quarrel between them. Both clans stood together on the need for expansion of Japan's empire into China, and the European war and the existence of the German colony of Kiaochow gave them their excuse.

Japan had 250,000 men under arms that August, organized into nineteen divisions. But including the reserves, she had 1,500,000 men available to fight, with another half million available each year for conscription under her universal military training laws.

She also had twenty-five battleships and cruisers and some sixty destroyers, and scores of gunboats and torpedo boats and service craft. She was ready for war, particularly when it was learned that the German East Asia cruiser squadron was not going to be augmented from Germany; instead the squadron was away from Asian waters and it seemed unlikely on 1 August that it would make the attempt to return.

On 2 August the Japanese government began to act. A message had been sent to London, noting that the Japanese Imperial throne was willing to put into effect the Anglo-Japanese alliance of 1911 if it came to the point. Baron Kato, the foreign minister, called British Ambassador Sir Conynghame Greene to the foreign office and handed him the note, which called particular emphasis to Article II of the alliance and one clause:

. . . if either of the High Contracting parties should be involved in war in defence of its territorial rights or special interests, the other High Contracting party will at once come to the assistance of its ally and will conduct the war in common and make peace in mutual agreement with it.

That clause was of particular appeal to the Japanese because it referred to special interests which were quite outside the matter of sovereignty. And Japan had a special interest in China: she wanted to control that land as she now controlled Korea and Formosa. If the British invoked the special interest clause and Japan entered the war, then Japan would acquire the special interests of Germany once she took over the German territory. It was all made for Japanese expansion.

That day Ambassador Greene called French Ambassador Eugene L.G. Regnault and Russian Ambassador Nicolas Malevsky-Malevitch and they promptly forgot their official manners long enough to bring their carriages to the British compound. The three ambassadors then met and discussed the Japanese offer. They were not unmindful of the dangers, of the Japanese ambitions in China. Malevsky-Malevitch was the most concerned, for his government had not long before engaged in a harsh and losing struggle against Japanese imperial ambition on the continent of Asia.

But Britain's short-range problem was tremendous. Ambassador Greene – Sir Conynghame in these surroundings – knew very well of the German plan for *Kreuzerkrieg* or cruiser warfare around the world. The dispatch of German colliers and freighters from Japan and China was well known to him already. The disposition of the German cruiser squadron was a partial mystery, but wherever the German warships were located, they must be presumed to be arming German fast passenger vessels as auxiliary cruisers for war against British ports. In those last scrambling days the vacationers in Tsingtao, sailing out on the coastal steamers *Kanschow* and *Ningpo,* had reported the arrival of a number of German ships in Tsingtao harbour. These must also be considered as dangerous vessels to British commerce and British interests. It was obvious to Sir Conynghame that his king's interests would be served best and fastest in the augmentation of the allied war effort by these thousands of Japanese troops and the hundreds of Japanese vessels that could control Asian seas and allow the British to send their forces westward where they were needed. Ambassador Regnault was not so sure.

The conferences continued for three days. Meanwhile the newspapers were filled with inflammatory material. The British Resident in Shanghai released a letter to the press, denouncing the Germans and their Austrian allies. The German Resident immediately replied. The communications were carried by all the papers of the Far East. Tokyo's newspapers featured them. In Tokyo other foreigners began expressing their views on the war, most of them attacking the Germans. It did not take long for feeling to reach a high pitch, particularly when this state of affairs was precisely what the emperor's ministers wanted.

Tokyo was still smarting from German 'interference' with Japan's machinations in China. At the end of the Sino-Japanese war of 1894 the Treaty of Shimonoseki had not only given the Japanese control of Korea, but Formosa, the Pescadores, and the Liaotung peninsula of Manchuria, including Port Arthur. Then, a few weeks later, the Europeans had reversed themselves and forced Japan to give up the Liaotung peninsula and her Manchurian claims.

Russia, Germany, and France had all been involved in the rescission demand; Japan was equally furious with all of them, but here was her opportunity to pay off the debt against Germany, and that was enough. For the German debt was greatest. Baron Kato and the others understood very well that the Germans had ambitions in the Far East. They knew that the Prussians were eager to turn the Czar's head from Europe to Asia, and that is why Germany had pressed to keep the Japanese from having Port Arthur.

It was complex. France played follow-the-leader: these affairs did not generally affect her interests in southwestern China. The French were not terribly eager to have Japan expand any further, yet they did not want to give too much ground to Britain even though they were now allies. So the ambassadors met all day long, and stayed up half the night sending messages home for instructions.

On 7 August the instructions were complete. Sir Conynghame visited the foreign ministry and suggested that Japan use her naval forces to augment the British Far Eastern squadron. The Japanese could help search out and destroy the German warships and capture the German merchant ships.

This almost passive role was not to the liking of Japan. No, she was not interested in being Britain's tame kitten in the Far East, pulling British chestnuts out of the Chinese fires. Japan was going to wage war against Germany!

In Tokyo German Naval Attaché Knorr was aware of the direction from which the wind was blowing, and he was doing everything in his power to force Japanese attention a different way. On the date of declaration of war by Britain, coming home with his prize to Tsingtao, Captain von Müller had encountered the Japanese ship *Sakaki Maru*. Von Müller had been very careful. He had radioed *Sakaki Maru* and sent visual signals, asking her to show her flag. And when she had showed the flag of the Rising Sun, *Emden* had saluted the Japanese vessel with a sweep of her war ensign, and sent her safely on her way.

Naval Attaché Knorr now issued a formal communique to the press giving the details of that encounter, and at the same time denying any wrongdoing by *Emden* and any ambitions against Japanese interests by Germany.

But it was no good. The opportunity for Japan to remove one of the troublesome European powers that interfered with her master plan for Asia was too great to pass up. Nothing the naval attaché or anyone else could have done would have made any difference.

In this atmosphere, on the night of 7 August, Count Okuma, the premier of the Japanese government, called an emergency meeting of the cabinet. It went on for four hours and did not finally break up until after 0200 hours.

The army spoke up. The navy spokesmen added their bits of advice. The political leaders of this non-political state discussed the needs of Japan. And everyone knew all the time what they were going to do: march into Shantung province and hold on to just as much new Chinese territory as they could take without arousing fury on the part of their allies.

On the morning of 8 August, then, Baron Kato was sent to the summer palace at Nikko to inform the emperor of the political and military situation that confronted the throne. In that way, if the emperor had strong feelings in some direction they could be ascertained; otherwise he could be expected to support the views of his subordinates.

That same morning, Vice-Admiral Yashiro, the minister of the navy, and Fleet Admiral Togo conferred on the readiness and capability of the Japanese fleet. They discussed the roles Japan's naval arm might have in extending the Japanese ambitions in the waters of the Far East, and how best Germany could be stricken there.

At the ambassadorial conference at the British Embassy Sir Conynghame had been given some straight talk by the Russians and the French, and he had transmitted it home. It had taken the government in London a bit of time to digest what was said, but on 8 August London was aroused enough to ask Sir Conynghame to persuade the Japanese to go slow. Sir Conynghame did just that, much to the annoyance of the Japanese foreign office. But it was essential that all being done be masked under the guise of 'obligations', lest Russia and France back away and start something in the Far East that would be most unpalatable to Japan. So Baron Kato fretted, but he listened to what the British ambassador had to say, and he indicated Japan's eagerness to please.

At least he listened until Sir Conynghame suggested that once Germany was driven out of Shantung province, the former colony of Kiaochow should be made a British protectorate.

That suggestion, even made unofficially, aroused Japan to sharp and immediate reaction. She was not going to enter the war against Germany to serve Britain's interests at the expense of her own, said Kato.

The mobilization of the army was called. From all over Asia, Japan ordered her transport ships home in the service of the government. Admiral Togo and Admiral Yashiro sent out orders that dispatched the vessels of the navy to Yokosuka naval base, and to Sasebo and Kure for provisioning and armament. Tight rings of security were thrown round these bases so no foreigner might be sure of what was happening there.

Britain's position was made official by a note from London suggesting that Kiaochow colony become British after it was captured. In fact, the British expected that they could capture the place with a couple of cruisers. They knew that Governor Meyer-Waldeck had fewer than five thousand defenders. They knew that the basic line of defence against any European attack would be the cruiser squadron. They knew by this time that plans had been made by the German government to use the cruiser squadron in some other manner – the dispatch of those colliers from Tsingtao and all the other points had not gone unnoticed by British agents in the East Indies, in Singapore and in Shanghai.

Japan balked. She would do nothing of the sort. Sir Edward Grey in London then considered the matter anew. Britain needed Japan and her ships. The *Rjasan* affair had already shown what those German cruisers could do to the shipping pattern if they were turned loose singly in Asian waters. They must be hunted down and destroyed, and there were not enough British warships on station for the task. Few if any could be spared from other areas and certainly nothing from the home fleet, as long as the German High Seas fleet stood opposite.

Sir Edward modified the British position. If Japan would enter the war, and would confine her operation to the China Sea, the British would agree to Japan's march on Shantung, provided Japan would also agree that 'eventually' Kiaochow would be turned over to China.

It was very easy for Japan to agree to do something 'eventually'. Eventually she intended to turn over all China to the status of Kiaochow, so that was the same thing was it not? There was no trouble here in the Japanese mind.

As for the British, they suddenly realized that Japan's rising to fulfil the treaty obligations was a potentially dangerous weapon against them. Germany's colonies in the South Seas could also be covered by Japan – it would be disastrous for British interests if the Japanese looked at Samoa, the Gilberts and Marshalls, and New Guinea as well. So Sir Edward hastened to confine Japan to China. What a few days before had been the unthinkable now became the preferable evil.

On 9 August the Japanese cabinet met in a long session to consider the British notes of recent days, and Baron Kato and Count Okuma expressed themselves satisfied with the manner in which affairs were proceeding. The emperor was notified, and then Baron Kato called in Sir Conynghame, and told him his government agreed to the terms suggested in the last British note. Japan was ready to go to war against Germany.

CHAPTER NINE

Threat to Tsingtao

On 9 August the German airways were busy. Count von Rex, the ambassador to Tokyo, had also been called to the Japanese foreign office that day. With a long face, Baron Kato had informed the count that it looked very serious – it was all unofficial of course – but it looked as though Japan was going to go to war against the German empire.

The count went back to the embassy and cabled Berlin and Tsingtao. Tsingtao was already under martial law, and had been since 3 August, two days before the break with Britain. There were no more European foreigners in the city to read the proclamations attached to the buildings, but there were some Japanese, and they were now notified of the ticklish situation of relations. They packed up and caught the trains to Tsinanfu, heading for Shanghai and the Japanese settlement there.

Tsingtao was in thorough confusion. Hundreds of Chinese had left the city by junk, by steamer, and by train. With the departure of *Emden,* and the rumours about the Japanese marching orders, hundreds more began to leave. Affairs grew so serious in the capital of Kiaochow that Governor Meyer-Waldeck had to put two hundred coolies under twenty-four-hour guard, to be sure he had the personnel to coal the ships that were leaving for the south.

All this was brought out on 10 August in Tokyo, when Count Okuma assembled the foreign journalists in Japan for a news conference. He dealt with the situation in Europe first of all. Then he told the newspapermen what was happening in Tsingtao. The Germans were arming the fortifications on the hills they called Mount Moltke, Mount Iltis, and Mount Bismarck. They had sent the freighters *Longmoons, Gouverneur Jäschke,* and *Staatssekretär Krätke* out into the Pacific laden to the gunwales with coal, to meet unknown and unpositioned German warships. The situation for all right thinking people was desperate.

Down south in Hong Kong, said the count, things were going the same way. British residents and visitors to the German colony had fled, and German residents of Hong Kong and British places were fleeing. All the British crews of the vessels in the Yangtse had been sent to British warships. British troops and sailors were on war alert at all times. The whole colony was seething with war activity.

The hundred newspapermen in Tokyo heard all that Count Okuma had to say and wondered when he was coming to the point.

One reason for his meeting, it was apparent, was to put down stories that the United States was very much concerned about Japan's coming entry into the war. Tokyo was full of rumour that day that the United States had officially notified Japan of its concern lest Japan march against the German colony. Count Okuma was taking this way of telling the United States, very politely, to mind her own business.

'How can the United States make such interference?' he asked angrily. 'Japan has done nothing in reference to the present war. Besides, judging from the behaviour of the United States and the traits of her people, no one will believe. . . .' (Even in those days of 1914 Japan had the idea that Americans would never, never fight.) Count Okuma tried to allay any journalistic fears that Japan's entry into the war would provoke America. He suggested that all those at his conference read a recent pacifist work by Congressman Hobson, before making such ridiculous noises about American intentions.

The importance of this press gathering was brought home when Lieutenant-General Oshima, the vice-minister of war, and Rear-Admiral Suzuki, the vice-minister of the navy and Vice-Minister Matsui of the office of foreign affairs all rose to their subjects. All spoke of coming war with Germany.

So the trial balloon was sent up, and Tokyo waited to see what would happen, particularly in Washington.

What happened was nothing, just as Count Okuma had suspected. The reports from Washington, and the messages, showed that America was indeed a huge paper tiger.

In all the hubbub one of the central reasons for holding the press conference at all went half unnoticed. It was the announcement by Count Okuma that in future the journalists were neither to seek nor print any information about the movement of troops of the army or vessels of the Japanese fleet. If they did so, the domestic newspapers would be suppressed, and foreign correspondents would be ejected from Japan.

That very day the torpedo boats *Kiji* and *Kamome* set out for Yokohama to stand outside and guard the harbour against any intrusions. The Japanese navy made no announcement, but from Yokosuka naval base Admiral Kato led out a fighting unit, which steamed out of harbour and turned south in the general direction of Formosa.

Japan was now swiftly transformed from an autocratic monarchy into a police state. Drastic censorship regulations were laid down on the press, so one might as well not read the newspapers at all to discover what could be happening in the war. During the next week half a dozen newspapers were suspended for speculating on the movements of troops and the fleet and the war situation in general.

All this while the emperor and his family spent the summer at Nikko, but on 15 August the Imperial family returned to the palace in Tokyo.

For a week the statesmen of Japan had been making ready for war. On 15 August the elder statesmen, a group of old and trusted noblemen who advised the throne on grave matters, assembled at the Imperial Palace with the chiefs of the general staff and the major admirals. They came to inform His Majesty of the state of affairs in Asia and to reaffirm the approbation they already had of their decision to take Japan to war. Statesmen and secretaries then prepared the Imperial Rescript.

In the interim, while the literary men worked, the emperor suggested that as imperial peacemaker and son of heaven it would be best if they gave Germany a chance to give up before making war on her. Surely the Germans must understand that they had not a chance of resisting the combined might of Japan and England?

So that evening, Baron Kato called Ambassador von Rex to the foreign office just after 1900 hours and with deep bows presented him with a note to the kaiser's government.

It was an ultimatum. Germany must first of all withdraw all her armed vessels from the waters of Japan and the China Sea. Any warships that could not easily be withdrawn must be disarmed. Germany then must hand over the colony of Kiaochow to the Japanese, without condition or compensation. If these conditions were not met, without argument, then at noon on 23 August the Japanese government 'shall take whatever steps it deems necessary'.

A sop was thrown to England in a phrase that indicated the Japanese seizure of Kiaochow was intended to enable the return of the colony to China. But it said no more, neither how nor when, and at least the Chinese and Germans were not fooled, even if the British pretended to be.

Thus was set up the machinery for a new Japanese incursion into China. More than that, the Japanese had firm designs on all the German colonies in the Pacific. They said nothing about the matter at the moment, but assuming an allied victory in the war, they intended to take their spoils and they knew precisely what these would be.

The Japanese ultimatum was received, as Count Okuma feared it might be, with considerable suspicion and misgiving around the world. The United States' opinion was negative in the beginning and this was important, for in spite of its isolationist policies the United States had become in twenty years a major industrial power, and all in Europe and Asia knew that if it

swung its weight one way or the other in the war it could tip
the balance. Without in any way sacrificing ambition, the Japanese were eager to keep the innocents in Washington pacified.

Count Okuma called another conference. This time he invited
a handful of newspapermen, but also the business and commercial leaders of the foreign community. He went to great lengths
at this meeting to assure the businessmen that Japan had no
reason other than her treaty with England to go to war with
Germany:

> Japan's object is to eliminate from the continent of China the root
> of the German influence which forms a constant menace to the peace
> of the Far East, and thus secure the aim of the alliance with Great
> Britain. She harbours no design for territorial aggrandizement nor
> entertains any desire to promote any other selfish end. Japan's warlike
> operations will not, therefore, extend beyond the limits necessary
> for the attainment of that object and for the defence of her own
> legitimate interests. Accordingly the Imperial government have no
> hesitation in announcing to the world that the Imperial government
> will take no such action as to give third Powers any cause of anxiety
> or uneasiness regarding the safety of their territories and possessions.

That very day Count Okuma sent a message to the Chinese
government in Peking, assuring China that all that was going
to happen was the fault of Germany and her 'aggressive actions'.
As usual, the aggressor was charging his victims with aggression.
The Chinese had by now accepted the existence of the German
colony in Shantung, and admitted that as colonists the Germans
were the most responsible and the most respectable who had
invaded China. They were not fooled by the Japanese words of
honey, and they were seriously distressed to learn the Japanese
intentions. President Yuan Shi-kai of the Chinese Republic
called his council of state into session, and there were many
discussions of the obvious plan of Japan to slice off another
piece of China, but until something happened there was nothing
to be done or even said.

The German ambassador to Peking thought there might be

some hope in the situation if Kiaochow could be transferred back to Chinese sovereignty. China would agree, certainly, and all that need be done was for Berlin to take swift action.

But Berlin was far more concerned with events in Europe. The war was going splendidly there: General von Kiuck's First Army had walked into Belgium and was driving swiftly towards Brussels and Antwerp. The French were about to mount an offensive around Metz.

The British were pouring across the channel to Le Havre, and Sir John French proposed to link up with the French at Le Cateau. So German attention was concentrated on the western front; the Austrians proposed to fight the Russians to the east, and there was very little attention paid in Berlin to the consideration of colonies in China.

In Tokyo Count von Rex went back to his embassy on the night of 15 August and sent the text of the ultimatum to Berlin. There was no doubt in his mind as to the outcome. Two days later he was supervising the burning of the embassy files and notes, and the embassy staff was packing up. War was inevitable.

In Tsingtao Governor Meyer-Waldeck received a long message from Berlin on the night of 17 August. In the end it said that he was to defend Kiaochow colony to the last, that was what his kaiser expected of him. There would be no capitulation to the insolent demands of Japan.

Then came Sunday, 23 August, and noon, the hour of expiration of the Japanese ultimatum. At the German embassy all was quiet. There was no message from Berlin, and Count von Rex had not expected one. The Japanese papers had already prepared their 'extras'. The clock struck twelve, and Count Okuma ordered his subordinates at the German section to prepare Count von Rex's passports. He telephoned the prime minister's office, and arrangements were made for the release of the Imperial Rescript. In a few moments it was humming along the wireless for transmission to the world. The 'extras' were released by the Tokyo papers, with the following on the front page:

We by the grace of Heaven, Emperor of Japan, on the throne occupied by the same Dynasty from time immemorial, do hereby make the following proclamation to all our loyal and brave subjects. . . .

And the gist of it was war.

Kiaochow was named in the rescript, and so were Japan's 'national aims', although no more about her aspirations was said than that. But reading between the lines, a foreigner could gather that Japan was going to war for reasons of her own that had nothing to do with the British treaty. And the die was finally cast.

CHAPTER TEN

The Defence of Tsingtao

In those tense days of July and early August, when it appeared certain there would be war in the Far East as well as Europe, Governor Meyer-Waldeck was given virtually no help at all from home. His force of regular soldiers and sailors consisted of only 1,600 troops. But from the moment of mobilization, all efforts in Asia were turned towards ameliorating the situation of Tsingtao. Admiral von Spee directed that the ships calling at Hong Kong and Nagasaki, Port Arthur, Taku bar, and all the other foreign ports in Asia bring with them men for the garrison of Tsingtao. Every man between the ages of eighteen and forty-five was a potential soldier of his kaiser, and they flocked in to serve, by ship and by rail through China, to Tsinan and then to Tsingtao. By the day of the Japanese Imperial Rescript there were nearly 4,500 of them, concentrated in the Moltke barracks and the other installations around the city, aware of their kaiser's orders to fight unto the death.

Like all in Tsingtao, *Leutnant* Gunther Pluschow knew their situation was hopeless. And yet that did not in the slightest deter him from heroic efforts to make his broken Taube fly. Quite to the contrary, the desperation of their situation freed him and the others from all restraint. They grew gayer rather than more sombre, braver rather than more cautious, as the situation became clear and they saw that their city and its tiny garrison was going to be the object of Japan's major attack in this war.

By 23 August the balloonists were expert at their work – Pluschow had seen to that. Poor *Leutnant* Mullerskowsky! Pluschow had warned him when the other was ready to fly. He had told him all he had learned about the treacherous currents of air that closed in on the racecourse airfield. He had shown him the drop off on the only clear side, over the hill and down to the bills below, with the sea standing sentinel at the end.

Mullerskowsky had listened, and he had paid as much attention as a man could when he was eager to be in the air, to test out the plane. He had taxied across the field and tested the currents, and taken off in the only direction one could take off on the field, over the end, above the cliffs and the sea.

It had been a downwind take-off, dangerous as could be with the single-winged Taube and its shaky stability. He had been caught in a downdraught at the end of the runway, and had plummeted to the rocks that guarded the bay. The Taube was a total loss, and Mullerskowsky was so badly hurt he had to be rushed to the hospital and surgery, after which he was propped up in a hospital bed with his arms and legs in plaster casts. No more flying for him this war.

As for Pluschow, he persevered. His Chinese friends found the kitemaker, and he came to supervise the rebuilding of the other Taube. Meanwhile Pluschow set his workmen to the task of building a biplane from scratch. He designed it, he supervised the whole construction, and the plane began to take shape.

The Taube took an immense amount of reconstruction. Silk had to be stretched across the patched-up framework. Then it had to be treated with a preservative and strengthener. The Chinese experimented until they found a lacquer mixture that would serve. Another big problem was the propeller. The Chinese workmen cut down seven oak trees to get straight pieces for the propeller, and fashioned a duplicate of the smashed one. They glued it artfully, and several days before the receipt of the Japanese ultimatum it was ready. The whole plane was prepared for testing in fact, and *Leutnant* Pluschow took her up. He managed to get off the runway, which was the most dangerous part until he came to land. He flew for several minutes, then, not wanting to test his luck too far, he brought her back, and made a perfect landing. But on inspection he discovered he had brought the

C*

Taube back in the nick of time, for his oak-tree propeller was about to come unglued. Another ten minutes in the air would have finished him – if he had been over the sea, it would have been goodbye to the plane and the pilot.

Pluschow consulted with his Chinese engineers. There was nothing that they could do. The glue was the best they could make with the materials at hand. It was just not strong enough to withstand the pressures of flight.

Well, said Pluschow, it would have to do. They must re-glue it, taking every precaution to make it as strong as possible. He would search around and see if he could obtain glutinous materials that would work better.

On the afternoon of 20 August, three days before the Japanese ultimatum expired with its declaration of war, Pluschow took off again with his re-glued propeller, and flew over the edge of Kiaochow bay to see if the enemy had yet sent its forces. He saw nothing except *S-90* going about her business of patrolling the harbour within the minefield. He flew back over the Shantung countryside, looking for signs of dust and moving horses and vehicles. Nothing. Pluschow came back to the airfield, landed safely, spoke to his mechanics, and headed down the hill to the governor's palace. He had just concluded his first successful reconnaissance flight, and he hoped for official commendation. But Governor Meyer-Waldeck was not impressed, for Pluschow had seen nothing, and yet that did not mean nothing was there.

Up on the hill, the mechanics took the propeller off the Taube, and moved in inside the shed they used as a hangar. The propeller was taken to a workbench, taken apart again, re-glued and put in clamps: these were Pluschow's orders and they would be carried out every day that he flew.

Back at the officers' club that day, Pluschow told the others of his experiences. There were not many left of the young crowd who were there in April when he arrived. *Oberleutnant* Schwartmann was still there, in command of the naval guns. One of the von Plissows was still in Tsingtao, Hans the aspiring aviator, but his twin brother Georg had been assigned to sail off in *Prinz Eitel Friedrich,* and after many encounters with the enemy would spend the remainder of the war as an internee and then a prisoner of the Americans, after *Prinz Eitel Friedrich* was taken into Newport News to avoid capture by the British. The officers Pluschow had known from gunboats *Tiger* and *Luchs* had gone with him to share the same fate.

All during August Governor Meyer-Waldeck had directed the training of the new men of the garrison as they came into camp and the arming of the city for its own defence.

Since Tsingtao lay on the little peninsula with Kiaochow bay west and south of it and the Yellow Sea to the east, they had three sea frontiers which meant the five thousand mines sown outside the harbour were the first line of defence. The land defence could concentrate on the north, past Fowshanso bay. Here the coolies and the troops were sent to dig entrenchments across the wide peninsula, between the rivers that bisected it, taking every advantage of the bits of terrain that lent themselves to defence. Actually that first line of defence was in discouraging country: the land was low and flat.

But behind the flat plain, and between that land and the city of Tsingtao lies Bismarck Hill and its lesser hills. Bismarck Hill is 433 feet high, standing in the centre of the peninsula with commanding views all around it, with an especially good view of the northern approaches.

The Germans had wisely chosen this spot at the outset of their rule as a major defence position, and so now as Meyer-Waldeck went to perfect the defences most of the work had been done for him. The fort stood tall and grey, built of reinforced concrete, in three sections that led down from the hilltop. It extended well inside the mountain, too. Placed at strategic spots were four eleven-inch howitzers that could throw a wicked fire of anti-personnel shells at an approaching enemy. Spotted around at various other locations were a number of four-inch guns that could fire against tanks and lorries, and could also be used to deliver shrapnel against infantry and cavalry.

The planners had done well. On the side facing Tsingtao the fort had tunnels and ammunition hoists, and on top there was an outlook with a fire control station buried in the rock. Inside, the hill tunnels had been hollowed to build kitchens and mess-rooms, sleeping quarters and storage facilities plus machine shops so that the engines of warfare could be repaired under fire.

Bismarck Hill, then, was the major German defence against land attack.

From the sea an enemy must first find his way through the minefield. If he could do that, he must then fight off the *S-90* and the old gunboats left to protect the city. If he could sink them, he had to contend with the fortifications around the city to protect it from sea attack. First was Huichuen Point, which stood a hundred feet above the sea, south of Bismarck Hill, sticking out into the bay. The fort here was built of solid concrete also, with searchlights and turret guns that could be withdrawn back inside the fortifications. The fort mounted two nine point four-inch guns and three six-inch guns, which made it almost the equivalent of a cruiser in strength. These guns were terraced inland in a line from the point to make them bear properly on the enemy and also make them harder to spot and hit.

Another battery was located at Iltis Point, and still another at Tuan Tao, at the end of the point that guards the wide bathing beach where the tourists from all over European China came for years to relax in the sun. Another battery was located behind the road leading to the beach.

All these defence positions were complete and manned with trained men and live ammunition before 23 August, the day of the expiry of the Japanese ultimatum to Berlin. For from the beginning, Captain Meyer-Waldeck had been expecting an attack of some kind by the British or the French.

Those two nations were moving with deliberate speed to try

to ascertain the whereabouts of various German units before
making their own concentrations. There were two basic British
units and two French units at sea in this half of the world. First
was Jerram's squadron based at Hong Kong. Second was Admiral
Patey's Australian command. Somewhere in the Pacific was
Rear-Admiral A.L.M. Huguet of the French navy, in his
flagship *Montcalm*, with another armoured cruiser and two lesser
vessels. The gunboat *Kersaint* and the cruiser *Dupleix* were also
somewhere about; the problem was to find them and coordinate
with them.

The British problem was complicated by the movements of
Admiral von Spee. No-one knew what he intended to do, but
the intelligence officers of Patey's staff felt he was about to launch
raids on Australia and perhaps New Zealand. Admiral Patey
concentrated most of his force near Sydney, for somewhere off
these waters he expected to meet von Spee. He set out to find
him and, if he missed, to go into Simpson harbour in Neu
Pommern and there destroy the German wireless station at
Rabaul.

But as soon as Patey began to move, he received the most
disconcerting messages about the movements of the German
fleet. In fact, von Spee was unswerving; he was moving his
various units to the relatively deserted Pagan, whence he would
move out towards Cape Horn and the Atlantic.

Admiral Patey tried to call up Admiral Jerram to suggest a
combined sweep of southwest Pacific waters to put an end to
von Spee. But Admiral Jerram was busy.

He had concentrated at Hong Kong, and had there been
found by the French ship *Dupleix*, which had joined up and
strengthened the squadron.

But Jerram was having tremendous problems. When the
battleship *Triumph* had been laid up and decommissioned at
Hong Kong, her whole crew had been discharged or transferred
to other duty. With mobilization and the recall of the ship to
active duty, Admiral Jerram had to get her fit to fight in a

hurry. The crews of the various Yangtse gunboats had been called south, and the gunboats laid up. But the crews of the gunboats did not make enough men to man the ship. It was suggested that *Triumph* be filled up with Chinese seamen, and it could have been.

But there was something mercenary about hiring Chinese, even though as citizens of Hong Kong they might be regarded as brothers of the empire. British thinking was not oriented quite that way in 1914.

The problem was solved by an appeal from Jerram to General F.H. Kelly, commander of the British military forces in South China. He allowed Jerram to call for volunteers to serve with the navy, and from the huge number of men who stepped forward two officers, a hundred other ranks, and six signalmen specialists were selected for *Triumph*. He hurried the details of getting her ready for sea, because he wanted to move up to Tsingtao and take action, possibly to capture *Emden*.

Such delays brought the situation into sharp focus – or so Jerram thought – and he learned that *Emden* was heading into the Pacific with a collier in tow. She was indeed. *Emden* and the merchant ship were going to meet Admiral von Spee at Pagan.

But Jerram felt *Emden* was more likely to be moving towards Yap, the big German communications centre in the south. This centre connected Tsingtao, Shanghai, and the Dutch East Indies with Rabaul and the Bismarck Archipelago. It would be useful to the allied war effort to have the Yap station destroyed. So Admiral Jerram set out to go to Yap first and then swing up to Tsingtao. He would take the cruisers *Minotaur*, *Hampshire*, and *Newcastle* to do that job, while *Triumph*, *Yarmouth* and *Dupleix* headed up to Tsingtao to establish the blockade.

All this was occurring in the early days of August. On the way south, Jerram captured *Elsbeth*, which had been sent out from Tsingtao with coal for the squadron. He ordered her destruction. Then he ran to Yap, and destroyed the radio station there by gunfire from his cruisers. The survey ship *Planet* had been sent to the island by von Spee, and her crew had just set up the defence garrison. But it was not much use to try to defend with rifle and machine-gun fire against the seven point five-inch guns of the British cruisers. The mast fell, the buildings burned, and the German defenders were left amid the ruins.

Then Admiral Jerram turned north, to assault Tsingtao if that seemed in order. He headed towards the Saddle Islands off the mouth of the Yangtse Kiang. There he would meet with the rest of his squadron and proceed north to blockade Tsingtao.

Admiral Jerram did not know it, but Captain Fitzmaurice, who was in charge of the *Triumph* and the other ships left behind, had very nearly caught Captain von Müller and the *Emden* a few days earlier. When von Müller steamed out of Tsingtao to reach the squadron at Pagan, he and the British had passed within a hundred miles of one another off Quelpart island.

Now Admiral Jerram set up his watch. The idea was to protect the Yangtse from German harassment and also to keep a good eye on Tsingtao so no one might go in. Jerram was relatively sure that all the important ships which had been in Tsingtao were gone, but he wanted to be sure that they stayed away.

By 10 August Admiral Jerram's squadron was very strong. It had been increased by the addition of the Russian cruisers *Askold* and *Zhemchug*. And Jerram's position had been strengthened by the word from the admiralty (which did not have to bother itself in the intelligence function with diplomatic niceties) that Japan was joining the war against Germany and that Japan would take over the protection of the Asiatic mainland and the sealanes adjacent to it. Admiral Jerram did not know it but the Japanese were already in action.

CHAPTER ELEVEN

Siege or Surrender?

The British were not so sanguine as to leave the whole job of protecting Asia to the Japanese. Captain Fitzmaurice and a strong section of ships were left behind to keep an eye on Tsingtao while Admiral Jerram and Admiral Patey went off to launch an expedition against the German colonies in the South Seas. It was just as well, as everyone knew, that this task was not left to the Japanese for reasons that were obvious in the whole Tsingtao situation. If Whitehall and Downing Street had been under even the slightest illusions about Japanese intentions, the manner of handling the German colony in Shantung had clarified the matter.

20 August, the day that *Leutnant* Pluschow took the renovated Taube up for its test flight and came back to report no action at all by the enemy outside the harbour, was the day on which the four remaining German merchant ships in Tsingtao harbour had chosen to sail. It was also the day on which Captain Fitzmaurice received more help in the form of *Dupleix Yarmouth,* and the *Empress of Asia* and was, for the first time since the blockade began, really able to block anything. Out sailed OJD *Ahlers,* which had been delayed, and *Senegambia, Frisia,* and C *Ferdinand Laeisz,* bound for various destinations to the south, carrying various cargoes.

Dupleix caught C *Ferdinand Laeisz* and *Senegambia* not far outside the harbour that very day. The French cruiser came up, fired the warning shots, and the captains of the German vessels had no recourse but to give up. How could they stand against an armoured cruiser?

Then out came *Frisia,* a five-thousand-ton vessel, carrying one hundred head of cattle, sixteen German officers, and $122,000 in gold bars (about £25,000, in those days). That was a prize to make the day of Captain Fitzmaurice and the men of *Triumph*. *Frisia* had no more chance to escape *Triumph* than the others had to run from the Frenchman.

These captures were so easy that when the Germans sent *S-90* out on her usual outside patrol on the morning of 23 August, the British caught sight of her, and decided to try to trap her. That evening, they knew, *S-90* would move back through the minefield to go into port. *Oberleutnant* Brunner knew what he was about; he did not know the ships he had escorted out just a few days earlier had been captured. He did know that Japan had now declared war against his country, and his mission outside this day had been to search for the Japanese fleet, and prepare Governor Meyer-Waldeck for what was coming.

S-90 moved slowly towards the harbour mouth on the evening tide, and Brunner was watchful and waiting, even if he knew not for what. Then, out of the setting sun, suddenly came smoke. An alert lookout aboard the *S-90* spotted the plume, and shouted to the world: *Rauchwolke!*

Oberleutnant Brunner issued orders, and his men swung into action. The word went down from the bridge to the engine room to give the ship every bit of power she had, for the vessel drawing up on them was a warship, no doubt of that. She was in fact the British destroyer *Kennet*, which had been scouting the area and had spotted the old German torpedo boat, which was slower and far less effectively armed than a British destroyer.

Cutting in fast, trying to get between *S-90* and the mouth of the harbour where the mines lay, the British destroyer opened fire, and in a few moments Brunner recognized her for what she was. He began returning the fire, and his gunners proved that in their time on the Yangtse, and in their days in Tsingtao, they had learned well from Admiral von Spee how to shoot. The *Kennet*'s fire was close, but *S-90*'s was murderous. One German shell knocked out one of the destroyer's guns, a fair hit right on target. The explosion killed three men outright and wounded six more so seriously that *Kennet* turned away before *S-90* reached the minefield (two of those men later died in the sick bay).

As darkness settled down on the China coast, *S-90* threaded her way through the mine-field her captain knew, while the British moved back to report to Captain Fitzmaurice on the adventure.

Tsingtao had been hit for the first time, and Tsingtao's men had drawn first blood.

But that day's action was only a beginning, as Brunner knew well, and so did Governor Meyer-Waldeck. There were congratulations that night ashore, when the torpedo boat came in with her brave tale of fighting the enemy and beating him. But there was no real celebration. The Germans knew that the beginning had come this very day with the declaration of war by the Japanese, and that they, a handful of men and a handful of ships and guns, were up against the full might of an army that had smashed China, and a navy that had beaten Russia to its knees a few years earlier. It was sobering matter for thought.

Many of the houses and establishments of Tsingtao were now closed down and boarded up, with the defenders concentrated to save fuel and food and be able to support one another quickly. Non-combatants had been ordered out of the colony in the first days of mobilization; this meant most of the women and children had left either to go to the international settlement of Shanghai, or to make their way by ship back towards Germany. Some women remained, and one of these was Sister Lena, a nun from Holstein, who was in charge of the emergency hospital set up at Prinz Heinrich guest house, a huge rambling stone structure on the bay.

On the afternoon of 23 August the Germans were ready, waiting for the attack they knew must come very soon. It did not come the next day, nor the next. But on 26 August, three days after the declaration of war, Admiral Kato brought the second Japanese cruiser squadron up outside Tsingtao. Meanwhile Captain Powlett of the British navy brought the cruiser *Newcastle* to the blockade region to represent British power. *Triumph* and one destroyer went to Weihaiwei, where they disembarked the troops who had enlisted in the ship's service at Hong Kong. Those men were destined to proceed to India to protect that land from any unrest during the European war. *Triumph* embarked some British troops for the fight against Tsingtao and returned to the scene where the action would take place.

Admiral Kato first landed a number of men on the islands at the edge of Kiaochow bay, where they set up a tent camp, and brought ashore provisions to establish a minesweeping base. Admiral Kato was well aware of the strong and dangerous minefield with which the Germans had surrounded their halfmoon bay. The Japanese cruisers *Suwo, Iwami,* and *Tango* were the principal fighting ships. At the moment, they had nothing to fight.

Drawing his force up in a semicircle around the bay, Admiral Kato made sure his blockade was as effective as it could be. Then he called in his chief of staff and dictated a new ultimatum, this one addressed to Governor Meyer-Waldeck in the German colony.

The Germans, he said, must receive a Japanese party under flag of truce, to discuss the conditions of surrender of the colony.

The message came into the communications centre and was transmitted to Governor Meyer-Waldeck in his office in the big administration building. He considered it, but only in the light of his orders from Berlin: he was not to give up the colony under any circumstances. Still, there could be no harm in stalling, playing the Japanese along, and perhaps gaining some valuable information about their attacking force that would make the defence more effective. The governor sent a wireless communication in return: he would be glad to receive a Japanese delegation as soon as the admiral told him what they wanted.

Vice-Admiral Kato received that message and he reacted swiftly. 'You are informed that the port of Tsingtao and the colony of Kiaochow are now under blockade,' he replied.

So the war entered its second phase for the handful of defenders inside the German city. It was to be a siege.

The five thousand defenders now redoubled their efforts to build defences on all sides of the city. The beach where so many pretty European girls had sunned themselves was strewn with barbed wire entanglements, in case the Japanese tried to land on the shores of the city by boat. Bomb-proof shelters were dug into the ground and the rock inside the city. Every machine-gun and every field piece available in the colony was brought to the port, to overlook the bay, or sent up to one of the hilltop fortresses that guarded the back of the city.

Meanwhile the Japanese army was already in action. Before the ultimatum was sent to Berlin, the army in Tokyo had acti-vated the units up north that would march on Tsingtao, and capture the German colony. The Japanese ambitions in Shan-tung province did not end here, although they must proceed with caution because the British had seized a piece of the peninsula for their naval base at Weihaiwei. Japan hoped to do as she liked with the German territory and extend her area of influence much further into Chinese territory, but she had to go slow lest she infuriate her new ally.

The Japanese moved slowly and methodically. All day long they swept along the minefield, trying to understand its character and configuration. The Germans had done a good job, the field held up. At night the ships stood insolently out at sea, lights flashing and flares signalling. But the Japanese did not attack or try to bombard the city.

One day Vice-Admiral Kato brought his cruisers up close, within the nine-mile zone that represented the effective range of the big guns on Iltis Point. Up went *Leutnant* Pluschow's barrage balloons to prove their worth, and the guns on Iltis

Point began to bark, with the loud deep noise of heavy artillery. Soon splashes were falling so close to the Japanese squadron that Admiral Kato gave the orders to turn away. If they had learned anything, it was that the Germans at Tsingtao knew their guns.

Soon the Japanese force was augmented by a little fleet of airplanes. The seaplane tender *Wakamiya Maru* was brought up and kept outside near the lighthouse, so the float planes could be used to spot German ships and installations in the harbour. Inside the Japanese found *S-90*, the old gunboat *Jaguar,* and the Austrian ship *Kaiserin Elizabeth,* which had already been prepared for scuttling.

Although Japanese planes began flying over Tsingtao the condition of *Leutnant* Pluschow's Taube was not such that he could either respond or go up to challenge them. Nor was he asked to do so. Captain Meyer-Waldeck was of the old school and nothing had changed his thinking – the airplane was at best a naval toy, and the proof of it was in the ineffectuality of the Japanese craft which created no more diversion than one of the Chinese kites.

But all this while the Japanese were moving, and finally on 3 September they landed a force of troops, more than 50,000 of them, on the Shantung peninsula at Lungkow, 150 miles north of the German city.

And then, a few days later, came the first effective enemy action: two of those contemptible Japanese seaplanes took off from their tender, and circling to gain altitude they headed for Tsingtao. They moved in high and flew over the city, dropped bombs on the railroad station and the big grey barracks, and killed several men and wounded others. First blood to the Japanese!

At Iltis Point and round the harbour the German pom-poms opened up and blasted away at the seaplanes, which now tried to escape through the blobs of grey and black smoke that indicated the exploding bursts of shrapnel. One plane was hit and hit again, and its pilot was wounded, but he managed, wobbling, to clear the area and in a long slow glide to make it back to the safety of the *Wakamiya Maru*, where the plane landed, the pilot was rescued, and the craft was hoisted aboard by crane for repairs.

In Tsingtao the wounded were then taken to the Prinz Heinrich hospital where Sister Lena and her crew of nurses put them to bed and cared for them, while the busy doctors of the garrison did what was necessary to save lives.

The seaplanes then became more aggressive. They were more stable and stronger craft than *Leutnant* Pluschow's badly weakened Taube. One of them was a Maurice Farman three-seat reconnaissance bomber. The Japanese had bought it from the French early in the year 1914 as an experiment. This was a good plane, thirty-one feet long with a wing span of sixty-four feet. It was powered by a seventy horsepower Renault engine; it could travel up to a height of three thousand metres, and could stay up for four and a half hours to observe the defences of the city and zero in on the naval guns of the cruisers. If necessary it could make a speed of about sixty miles an hour, although top speed cut down its endurance.

Earlier the Japanese had bought three Maurice Farman two-seater seaplanes, and two of these were the planes that bombed Tsingtao for the first time. They were not quite as large or fast as the three-seater and could stay up only three hours at a time.

Now, with the Japanese planes flying, spotting and occasionally bombing, the harbour at Tsingtao rang with the fire of the guns, and the feeling of war hung heavy in the air.

When Governor Meyer-Waldeck learned of the landing of the Japanese land forces to the north, he immediately dispatched three units of German troops to the edges of Kiaochow to scout and determine the character and intentions of the enemy force coming down the peninsula. One detachment was sent to Chin chia kow, to guard the road that led down from the Chinese city of Chih Fu. A second detachment went to Kaomi, to scout and stop if possible the Japanese advance on the road from Lungkow.

The third detachment was sent to Chu Cheng to guard the southern seacoast and prevent a surprise landing.

The war was coming ever closer to the city itself.

CHAPTER TWELVE

Siege

The troops sent out to reconnoitre soon sent back word to Tsingtao that explained the slowness of the Japanese advance. That month heavy floods had hit the northeastern end of the peninsula, and the rivers had become torrents; even the creeks had swollen and burst their banks. The Chinese roads were seas of mud, in which the Japanese lorries and wagons were bogged down so that teams of horses had to be brought in to pull them out.

Governor Meyer-Waldeck took stock of the colony's situation. It was impossible, of course, given continuation of the war in Europe. But it was not desperate in the immediate future. The Japanese in the north were a long way away. The Japanese outside the harbour were going to stay outside for a long time – the minefield made that much certain. As for the town itself, it was in excellent shape.

When the planners laid out Tsingtao they had followed the old German architecture but they had one great advantage over German cities; there were no old alleys and streets to be dealt with, no crookedness and slum or ghetto. So the wide streets had been laid out in rectangular patterns, with large gardens and squares – plenty of living space. That meant a Japanese bomb or shell, even if it hit a stone building and started a fire, was not going to begin a conflagration the way bombing or shelling of a European city would do. From the railroad station, Prinz Heinrich, Kronprinzen and Hohenzollern Streets still ran, uncluttered, down to the heart of the town. The police station at the head of Berliner Strasse was untouched by bombs. And all around, Governor Meyer-Waldeck had his six hundred Krupp guns to protect the people.

The Japanese continued to mass troops in China – a violation of the neutrality of China, and an action seen in Peking for what it was: pure Japanese expansionism. China was too weak to do much about it, but the government officials were wise enough to keep the British and French in Peking informed, and to make protests which would show the world what was happening. Bearing the yoke of foreign imperialism, the Chinese must exhibit subtlety.

Early in September the Japanese began to move beyond Lungkow, and their eyes were on the railroads. But on 4 September the Chinese in Peking sent the Japanese legation a stiff note about the violations of Chinese territory in the march against Kiaochow-leased territory. China would have to let the Japanese march against Kiaochow, said the note, but let the Japanese beware:

The Chinese government will not accept responsibility for the passing of troops or any war operations at Lungkow, Laichow, Kiaochow, and their adjacent districts, but in the other districts of China the government will strictly enforce neutrality as declared. The territory and diplomatic negotiations of China are recognized by the Powers and they will likewise protect the property of the inhabitants in the region to be affected by the war operations.

So Japan was warned. Her alliance with Britain would definitely be threatened, for the Chinese would call on Britain in her own interests to prevent Japanese ingressions.

But the Japanese went just as far as they could. On 11 September they entered Tsimo, ninety miles from Lungkow. Their pretext was that the other routes to Kiaochow were flooded. The next day they began the move towards the muddy, flooded roads toward Weihsien, and once again were outside the territory in which they were allowed to operate.

That was only the beginning. The Japanese now fanned out and seized the Shantung railroad, a straight violation of China's sovereignty. They began shooting down Chinese officials and workers who protested. It was not long before they took various towns along the railroad, and pushed on to Tsinanfu, the capital of the province and the head of the rail line. It was apparent that the Japanese intended to seize all of Shantung if no one stopped them.

Pingtau was not very far from Tsimo, where the Germans maintained a garrison of a dozen men as lookouts for the enemy. The Japanese reached Pingtau on 11 September. Hearing that the Germans had garrisoned Tsimo, they sent out cavalry the next day, and behind them came the infantry marching toward Tsingtao.

The small German military detachment at Tsimo was armed only with light guns, but when the Japanese came up on 12 September they began firing. In the action that followed two of the Germans were wounded, and the garrison evacuated, leaving a city of 30,000 in the hands of the Japanese.

The word that the Japanese had moved almost to the edge of Tsingtao's vital zone reached Captain Meyer-Waldeck. He had plenty to think about, for the planes from the seaplane carrier bombed Tsingtao that day, and put three big holes in the tile roof of the Moltke barracks, and more holes in the roof of the governor's palace.

Japan moved slowly, with the leisurely air of a gentleman strolling down the street. Why not? The Germans were not going anywhere, and it was unthinkable that the enemy could be reinforced. It was known that the admiralty in Berlin had other plans for Admiral von Spee – and it was generally believed that he was probably on the other side of the world by this time.

So after the capture of Tsimo, instead of rushing forwards the Japanese military commanders and their staffs took time to have tea with the mayor and officials of the town, and to visit the Buddhist temple and Confucian shrine to show their respect for the people and their ancestors.

As the sun came out and the weather cleared, the Japanese busied themselves by bringing up supplies to Tsimo on the edge

of the Kiaochow district. They moved then to Laushan, which
was just fifteen miles from Tsingtao. Laushan was a sheltered
place, situated on a little bay that would let some ships and
lighters bring in supplies, and located at the foot of the Laushan
mountains that protected Kiaochow. The Japanese were moving
to establish a blockade and a siege, that much was certain.

On 14 September Japanese Commander Aoki, who was in
charge of the destroyer flotilla under Admiral Kato, was ordered
to make a reconnaissance of Laushan bay. Potentially, it was a
dangerous mission, because the Germans just might have fortified
this bay or laid mines as they had all around Kiaochow bay.
Commander Aoki welcomed the chance for glory, and set out
on his task; there was nothing in the area but a handful of
German military sentinels, who were driven back from the hills
by the landing force. The destroyers held the bay, soon they
brought in minesweepers and support ships, and before the week
was out a series of Japanese transport vessels arrived, and began
to make preparations to unload 15,000 men who would partici-
pate in the siege of the city. Huge siege guns came off the
transports into lighters, and were hauled up the beach and to the
mountains. Behind them came boatloads of ammunition and
supplies, field kitchens, hospital units – everything that would
establish the army on this side of the beleaguered city.

There was flat ground suitable for landing and take off of
landbased planes, and here the Japanese army brought its air
force. The Japanese army's air force was the strongest air power
on the Chinese continent at the time.

The Japanese planning had been as thorough as it could be.
In the summer of 1914 when the general staff learned through
its agents in Tsingtao that the Germans had brought in the two
Rumpler Taubes, they moved swiftly to purchase a pair of those
machines for themselves. This was before the war broke out.
Further they secured delivery, and they brought hoseplanes to
the Far East – all in a matter of weeks. But their major air force
was French in design and manufacture, for the French in 1914,

and throughout the war, for that matter, were excelled in their airplane design only by the Germans. The Japanese had four 1913 model Maurice Farman biplanes, with seventy horsepower Renault engines, four hour endurance time at a speed of fifty-five miles an hour. They also had one 1913 Nieuport NG 2 monoplane, a two-place ship powered by a Gnome one hundred horsepower engine. It was the fastest thing in the air at nearly seventy miles an hour.

The Japanese settled in here and prepared for the eventuality of siege. They did not expect it, they hoped to bring their artillery and cavalry up to the gates of Tsingtao and secure a surrender by show of force. General Mitsuomi Kamio, the Japanese commander, was a careful man however, and he made ready for any eventuality.

One of the first tasks came from the lessons learned in the landings – the Chinese countryside was subject to floods, and the roads were then impassable. So a railroad must be built to carry heavy equipment to the front. It was begun, using Chinese coolie labour. It would be a narrow gauge railroad, of the kind often used in the Far East, because it was easier to construct than the broad gauge kind.

The Japanese had now cut Tsingtao off from land communication with Chinese cities. The Japanese army had invested nearly all the towns along the Shantung rail line and had taken the Chinese city of Kiaochow. The cable line from Tsingtao to Shanghai had been cut. The big wireless station remained and kept Governor Meyer-Waldeck in touch with the outside world and with Berlin.

The Japanese were aware of the existence of the big radio station. It depended on its tall transmission tower, and both naval and army planes tried at various times to destroy it. One bombing raid did knock the tower down, but the lightness and simplicity of a radio tower was such that the Germans had it back in operation within a few hours.

On 18 September the Japanese had completed all their advance preparations and were ready to move in the attack on Tsingtao. That day General Kamio ordered an advance, and from Laushan came a large force of Japanese army troops. They moved along the rolling countryside for eight miles outside Laushan, until they came to the foothills, and here ran smack into a detachment of one of the German infantry battalions, armed with machine-guns. The Germans stopped them for several hours. The Japanese advanced under fire cover, the Germans replied, the Japanese stopped. But eventually they put flankers out so far that the German defenders were in danger of being outrun and captured. Then and only then did the Germans retreat stubbornly and reluctantly. They moved back to Tsingtao, contesting every piece of ground where they could hold for a little while.

The Japanese cavalry came out scouting that day, moving from Kiaochow along the river Pai Sha toward Liu Ting. Here they met a German force led by Baron Leadsell, a volunteer who had been second secretary of the German legation at Peking before the call for volunteers and reservists rang through the Far East. They fought, the Germans and the Japanese, and Leadsell was killed in the engagement. So was Captain Zenji Sakuma of the Japanese cavalry.

The Germans divided their defence forces into five battalions of infantry with a few cavalry scouts, five battalions of marine artillery, and twenty-five hundred reserve officers and men who could be used to bolster various forces. The infantry took basic responsibility for the maintenance of the outer defence lines, where these skirmishes were being fought. The artillery men took responsibility for the defence of the city from naval and air attack.

The action in mid-September was on the outskirts of the city north and east of Tsingtao. Here the superior Japanese forces were steadily pushing the German defenders back to the fortress line – but not without a contest over every yard of ground. For two weeks the Japanese pushed forwards in the mountains south of Laushan. Their constant pressure made the Germans move back toward Tsingtao, and on 22 September the Japanese won control of the highest point of ground in the area, San Piao Shan, a mountain nine hundred feet high. From here their artillery could dominate the plain and the rugged lands below. From here, too, their artillery spotters could maintain a watch on the German reserve line, at Litsun, four miles away. That line ran from Litsun to Sha Tse Kau.

The Japanese were moving along at about the speed General Kamio had expected. Now they were joined, on 24 September, by a British force of slightly less than 1,300 men, comprising the Tientsin garrison of the South Wales Borderers, and a detachment of Sikhs.

On 26 September the Japanese and the British attacked together on the high ground that stands between the rivers Pai Sha and Li Tsun. The fighting was vigorous but, as always, the Germans could not commit enough troops to do more than hold for a time, and they were forced back so that the allies occupied the right bank of the Li Tsun the next day. They were now only seven miles northeast of Tsingtao.

For some time the Japanese had been harrying the city with their airplanes. Their bombing was sporadic and not very accurate, but it was almost daily, and that did interfere. More bombs were dropped on the Moltke barracks, and more struck the governor's palace, as the allies tried in vain to wipe out the radio communications system with Yap and Berlin. One Japanese plane managed to put a bomb into the *Kaiserin Elizabeth*, and started a fire aboard the Austrian vessel, but the crew rallied and the fire was extinguished before it did any serious damage.

Brigadier-General Barnardiston, the commander of the British forces, led his men into battle that week, and they helped the Japanese in their movement up and down the line.

For some days *Leutnant* Pluschow had been refused permission to fly the Taube over the enemy lines, although he had applied again and again. Governor Meyer-Waldeck simply did not believe the airplane could be of any use to him. But after the capture of Kiaochow, which gave the enemy control of the railroad twenty-two miles away, and the right bank of the Li Tsun, which brought them even closer, Governor Meyer-Waldeck was willing to listen to the lieutenant's suggestions, particularly when Pluschow claimed he could spot the enemy's changes in position for the artillery.

So Pluschow went to the airfield and started up the engine of the little plane. Meyer-Waldeck had cautioned him about one thing: he must fly in the late afternoon, just as dusk was falling, when the enemy would be unable to bring its guns to bear on him so quickly and he might possibly escape being shot down.

So Pluschow went up, and he scouted the roads and the positions of the enemy. The Japanese were moving steadily forwards on the Li Tsun front, and soon reached the river Chang Tsun. Here they were little more than five miles from Tsingtao.

Pluschow came back that night of his second mission and drew for Meyer-Waldeck a plan of the enemy position and movement. The captain was very much impressed, and he thereupon gave permission for Pluschow to conduct regular flights over the enemy lines for observation purposes only.

The Japanese and British were very badly informed about the German 'air force'. They believed it consisted of several planes. The fact was that the Taube was unarmed, and there was not a single aerial bomb in the whole German colony. Since the Japanese planes were armed and had bombs, they did not think the Germans would be less well equipped, and consequently Pluschow got more respect when in the air than he really deserved.

Pluschow had two areas of responsibility. He was to check the movement of troops and the concentration of materials on the ground, and he was also to keep track of the enemy sea forces. His flights over the attacking cruiser squadron caused the Japanese and British to keep moving their ships, lest the Germans send out warships to strike them at night. Every night Admiral

Kato changed the anchorage. Every day the Japanese and their British allies steamed along the coast, outside the line of the minefield, which they had been unable to penetrate well enough to sweep clean.

Inside Tsingtao, the feeling that a siege was imminent had begun to seize the inhabitants of the city. The bombing in particular made them aware of the dangers they all faced. They clustered together in a few of the big houses, to save food and fuel as well as to gain strength through companionship. The missionaries maintained their own place but soon moved to the hospital to be of help. Mission Superintendent C.A. Boskamp brought his wife and his sons Hans and Martin, and Professor Richard Wilhelm to the place. Also Sister Strecker came to work there. On Sunday, 20 September, they conducted religious services, ending with the song of David.

That week the war came home to the Germans in another way. *Leutnant* von Riedesel was brought in wounded, along with three enlisted men. They were treated by the doctors and put to bed in the big bright rooms of the former guesthouse. The war had most certainly arrived in Tsingtao.

Leutnant Pluschow learned something new about the war that week. In previous flights he had been aware of a certain amount of fire directed against his plane, but the anti-aircraft guns of the Japanese and the British were not a great danger, as long as he stayed away from the ships, and he was not seriously worried about them.

Then, just at dusk at the beginning of that week, he went out to find the enemy troops, and dived down low over a column of men moving up from the rear to the front line so close to Tsingtao. He saw puffs of smoke and knew that the men below were firing at him. But not until he landed and inspected the Taube did he realize how well they were firing. He counted ten bullet holes in his airplane, and promised himself not to be quite so daring in the future.

Night after night now Pluschow went up to check the enemy.

Governor Meyer-Waldeck was glad to have him for the reports he was receiving about the amount of ammunition available to his guns were disturbing. The garrison could not hold out long, and every shell must be made to serve its purpose if it was to hold out at all.

The Germans had one weapon that was most effective in keeping them informed: the loyalty of many of the Chinese servants and Chinese Christians in the Kiaochow community. These Chinese slipped through the lines, night after night, and scouted the Japanese enemy and brought back information to the missionaries, who promptly reported to Governor Meyer-Waldeck and the defending garrison.

Day by day the fighting continued, and every afternoon and evening more men were brought to the old guesthouse for treatment of their wounds. On 24 September, the Japanese bombed the city heavily, making a number of forays against the town. Five bombs struck in the harbour area, starting fires and smashing into several godowns. Two struck in the courtyard of the Bismarck barracks, doing little damage but reminding the men of the enemy's power.

On 25 September, a German patrol surprised a detachment of Japanese on the northwestern front, and captured a number of Japanese newspapers. Translated, these gave the Germans a good idea of the importance with which the Japanese were investing this war: photographs of the Japanese forces on the front page, and a number of articles from the front and the naval blockaders.

That day nine bombs fell on the city.

On 26 September, the floods in the northeast had abated so that the Japanese heavy transport could make use of the roads again. The Japanese were on the move. The constant overflying of the city and the military positions in the north was bringing new trouble to Governor Meyer-Waldeck. For what Pluschow could do with his little Taube, the Japanese could do almost ten times as well with their airplanes. And the

D

preponderance of power was beginning to tell in every way.

The Japanese moved forward until they almost completely surrounded the fort on Bismarck Hill. Surrounding, of course, and taking were two different things. The fortress stood up above, its guns pointed down, and the Japanese must move slowly and cautiously as long as those guns remained. The planes they had, primarily observation planes, would never be capable of dislodging the big siege guns in the fortress.

On 26 September, Governor Meyer-Waldeck decided to give the enemy something to think about at sea. He brought out *S-90*, the old gunboat *Jaguar*, and *Kaiserin Elizabeth*, and moved them up the bay of Kiaochow, close in between Huechuen Point and Iltis Point, so they could throw shells at the Japanese troops advancing northeast of Bismarck Hill. The fortress and the ships threw a heavy fire on the enemy, and stopped their movement forward. But the Japanese soon launched a counterattack, in the form of bombers. The planes took off, each carrying several bombs, and dropped them around the German ships, coming so close that the captains of the vessels decided to move out of the area.

On 28 September, the allies moved forward again, and after some heavy fighting pushed their way to a hill point only two and a half miles from Bismarck Hill itself. Here they stopped at noon. To go forward further would mean to launch a major offensive against the fortress, and this was going to take some planning.

A detachment of destroyers and light ships was separated by Admiral Kato, and instructed to move into Fowshanso bay, on the northeastern side of Iltis Point and outside the minefield, to give support to the British and Japanese troops as they moved forward. Particularly the ships were to prevent any recurrence of the German dispatch of their naval forces to engage against the troops. The destroyers and other ships moved into the bay at the foot of the Laushan range, and turned their four- and five-inchguns against the positions outlined for them by the spotters from the airplanes. They helped roll up that German line on 28 September, in which four old field guns were deserted by the defenders. They had lost very little: only these pieces that were relics of the Franco-Prussian war.

The Japanese and British now became bolder, hoping to make a single great strike that would end the German defence. The Taube bothered them a great deal, so that evening they decided to put an end to it. Waiting until late in the day, when they were sure the Taube would be out on the field, preparing to take off, the Japanese sent a flight of planes against the racecourse.

The plane was outside its hanger on one side of the little field. The Japanese had been quite right.

Pluschow was there, and heard the sound of aircraft approaching. It could be nothing but enemy, that he knew, and then '. . . a giant biplane shot out of the clouds right over our heads. I was speechless. As one entranced I looked at the spectre, and now I noticed the big red balls on the under side of the wings of the airplane. So, a Japanese.'

Soon the bombs began falling. Fortunately not one came close enough to damage the Taube. But the lesson was obvious, and that very night Pluschow put his Chinese workmen and enlisted men to the task of building another hangar across the field, while the first one was completely camouflaged – badly. The new hangar was camouflaged, but well. And the Chinese workmen built a dummy Taube out of light wood, and put it in the old hangar. Every day it was brought out and displayed on the field, while the real plane was hidden away except when it was actually to be used in flight.

The Germans were making do with what they had.

CHAPTER THIRTEEN

Under Pressure

The Japanese and the British kept moving on and consolidating their positions. It was too bad, but a day or so after the move to the foot of Bismarck Hill, Governor Meyer-Waldeck ordered the burning of Meaklenberg Inn. What a waste! This handsome mountain inn, designed in the fashion of the Bavarian resorts, had been a favourite spot winter and summer of Tsingtao's residents, and a target for the mountaineering types who liked to climb the hills. Not only was the inn burned, but demolition teams went out to destroy all the bridges across the mountain gorges, for they might possibly be used by the enemy to bring artillery up to command the fort on Bismarck Hill.

German raiding parties also went out into the countryside under cover of darkness and blew up the railroad bridges and trestles between Tsingtao and the edge of Kiaochow colony, to prevent the Japanese from using the Shantung railroad to bring supplies up to the edge of the city for siege.

Admiral Kato hoped he could put an end to Tsingtao once and for all by destroying the minefield and then bringing in the cruisers and battleships to bombard the fortress and the town into surrender. The trouble at the moment was that the carefully laid minefield kept the big ships out of range. So every day minesweepers and trawlers went out to try to find the mines. On 30 September the sweeping operation cost them dear. Two Japanese minesweepers hit mines that day and went down, with heavy loss of life. The operation was suspended, and for a time the navy let the army carry the battle against Tsingtao.

The Japanese and British were very thorough. They cleared the whole countryside north of the Tsingtao forts and made

sure there were no pockets of resistance before they spread out
their line about the beleaguered city. The advance was slow and
very costly, for the Germans, from their higher positions, raked
the enemy troops with constant harassing fire that was sometimes
quite effective. The Japanese, then, were reduced to building
trenches below the hills and while these trenches protected them,
they also immobilized the Japanese army and gave the Germans
a point of aim.

Leutnant Pluschow's daily flights became ever more important
to Governor Meyer-Waldeck in his placement of his meagre
defences. Each day Pluschow flew out to see what was changing,
then came back to his little field, landed, and was rushed by
staff car to the governor's palace where he spent the next few
hours briefing the commanders and working over the situation
map to show the changes.

He began flying mornings as well as evenings, but was soon
faced with the shortage of gasoline that threatened his whole
operation. He considered methods of cutting down on fuel
consumption. His home made propeller was too small for the
plane, and the Taube was thus hard to handle. It became harder
to handle when he stripped the plane of all unnecessary gear,
which included seat covers and anything that could be removed.
He even flew without a jacket so that the weight would be less.

As the Japanese surrounded the city, the airfield became a
primary target for their artillery. Every time the plane took
off, the enemy guns fired at it constantly while it was in the air,
and when the plane landed on the field where it was out of
sight of Japanese observation points, they fired blindly at the field,
and at the road which they had zeroed in from aerial observations
of their own. So the daily routine became for Pluschow to take
off, and almost immediately be harried by puffs of artillery fire
around him, to carry out his observation mission, which meant
making notes while flying the plane – all the while those black
and grey puffs rising about him – and to return to the field,
pursued by Japanese gunfire, and sometimes by Japanese planes.

Pluschow was under strict orders to refrain from engaging the Japanese planes, for he was the only aviator capable of flying and his plane was the only one capable of taking the air. He would land, then, and jump into the staff car, and speed down the hill, trying to avoid the shellholes in the road, and hoping that the Japanese did not get lucky and plant a shell on top of him as he moved on the perilous track to the city.

Most of Pluschow's flights were carried out against the army forces on the land side, but from time to time he scouted the naval force outside the minefield. One day he was out flying around the cruisers when he looked up to see a Japanese seaplane above him. Just as he looked up he saw a small form detach itself from the plane and head down. A bomb!

Pluschow dived off to the right and the bomb missed. The Japanese followed the manoeuvre and dropped another missile on him. Pluschow evaded that one too, and headed home for the racecourse and the protection of the Krupp guns around the city. Looking back he saw that he was trailed by two Japanese planes, not one, but his one hundred horsepower Mercedes was faster than their engines and he got away. The Japanese followed him home, but turned back when they reached the outskirts of the city, peppered by flak from the guns below. By now, having been hit several times, the Japanese pilots had a fine respect for the Germans and their armament.

The Japanese soon launched a serious campaign to knock the Taube out of the sky, for General Kamio realized that the plane's observations were the key to the German defence. Each time the Japanese and the British would move their field guns, within a matter of hours the Germans would have the position and range and be firing on them. The British camp was notable for its clean white tents, and Pluschow found those soon enough and the Germans conducted a bombardment of the headquarters that, while not disastrous, caused Brigadier-General Barnardiston to move the whole operation out of range.

So the army planes lay in wait for Pluschow and tried to

ambush him. 'When I spotted one of my enemy army colleagues close below me,' said Pluschow, 'I gave chase and fired down on him, firing thirty shots from my paragellum pistol.' The Japanese plane fell off sharply and headed for the ground, hit somewhere. It descended very rapidly and crash-landed in a field. The pilot survived, and apparently the plane was saved, but Pluschow achieved a kind of notoriety for being one of the earliest aviators on any front to score a victory in plane-to-plane combat in the air.

Pluschow had no bombs, but the armourers of the Tsingtao garrison undertook to make some for him. They found coffee cans and loaded them with explosives, nails, and scrap iron.

Pluschow went out one day with a handful of bombs in the cockpit, and found himself a Japanese destroyer. He came in low, plastered one of his bombs on the deck of the ship, and then looked back. It had been a dud. He tried another. It was a dud. He jettisoned the rest and went home to Tsingtao to report disgustedly to the armourers that they had better improve their workmanship.

They did. Within a few days Pluschow was out with another batch of coffee-tin bombs. He found a Japanese column moving down a road behind the front, dropped two of his bombs on the troops, watching with immense satisfaction as they went off and created both casualties and tremendous confusion among the enemy. Those two effects were about the best the Germans could expect; there was no question in the minds of any persons in or outside Tsingtao that the fortress city could stand forever. True, in late August and September there were hopes in Tsingtao that the German armies before Paris might capture the French city, and force an end to the war on the western front. But only thus, through a general victory (which for a time seemed very possible), could Tsingtao stand. And by October, with the Battle of the Marne ended in stalemate, and the French and British holding on tenaciously at Verdun, it was apparent that the war in Europe was not going to end so quickly.

Tsingtao was doomed and everyone knew it. Yet Governor Meyer-Waldeck had his instructions to hold out, and he was determined to resist just as long as possible.

Early in October, General Kamio decided that he would press the attack and get it over with in a hurry, even if it meant losing more men than he would by a long slow siege. He stepped up the movement of his troops, his artillery began to thunder, and outside the mine barrier, the Japanese and British vessels moved in as close as they could and then began bombarding the various points of resistance. Governor Meyer-Waldeck responded with his own artillery. General Kamio and Admiral Kato took stock at the end of three days and found the German defences were far from overwhelming, so they decided on the frontal assault that month.

Chinese observers on the scene were now telling Peking that it was all over for the Germans, and so the government in Peking had slowed its protests against the Japanese investment of the Shantung railroad and many cities outside the German protectorate. On 3 October, in preparation for the assault, the troops of General Kamio took over the Shantung railroad from Tsinan Fu to Weihsien. But the Germans paid no attention to the Japanese manoeuvres, other than to mine the railroad, so that a Japanese train was destroyed as it tried to bring supplies in from the outside.

General Kamio expected that it would take him only three days to reduce Prince Heinrich Hill, the first fort in line. So he brought up his siege guns in the early days of October and planted them round the hill. While the Japanese were making these extensive preparations, the Germans did not increase the activity of their own big guns, a fact so remarkable to General Kamio that it caused him to become overconfident and commit himself prematurely. On 8 October, expecting an easy victory, the Japanese began to move up on Prince Heinrich Hill. Governor Meyer-Waldeck, knowing his own potential reserves and his ammunition supply, had already decided to sacrifice that position without more than rearguard action, so General Kamio was again surprised when his men virtually walked up Prince Heinrich Hill without opposition.

The Japanese were jubilant. They now discounted all they had heard before about the 'last ditch defence' the Germans would make at Tsingtao. They had expected a series of Banzai charges, of the kind they themselves would have staged, to destroy as many of the enemy as possible from a hopeless position. And there had been no charges at all – the German defence was slackening instead of stiffening.

General Kamio's intelligence officers had been listening in on the German communications. A few days earlier, Tsingtao had received a very long message from Berlin, in code. The Japanese had not broken the code, but they speculated on the contents of the message, and General Kamio came to the conclusion that the governor of Tsingtao had just received detailed instructions from Berlin on the course of surrender of the colony. Why else could they have taken Prince Heinrich Hill in one day with almost no casualties?

The next two days were occupied by the Japanese in hauling siege guns up the hill, so they could fire upon the interior German positions. General Kamio also sent a wireless message in the clear in German to Governor Meyer-Waldeck:

The undersigned have the honour to convey to your Excellency the most gracious wishes of the Emperor of Japan, who desires to save non-combatants of the belligerent country as well as the subjects of neutral countries at Tsingtao who desire to escape from the loss that may arise from the attack on the fortified port. If your Excellency desires to accept the proposal of the Emperor of Japan, you are requested to furnish us with a detailed communiqué about it.

Lieutenant-General Kamio
Vice-Admiral Kato

This message came in on the night of 10 October. Next day Governor Meyer-Waldeck ordered that it should be circulated throughout the community, with especial attention to the

D*

foreigners who remained in Tsingtao and the missionaries of all faiths and nations including the Germans.

A dozen people decided to leave. All of them were non-combatants. Among them was Consul-General Peck of the American foreign service, who had remained until now on orders of his government. But Consul-General Peck, having informed the legation at Peking of the situation from day to day, was now ordered by his superiors to come out while he still could. There was no further peaceful aim to be pursued in Tsingtao, and there was considerable danger to the consul if he remained.

So on the night of 11 October, Governor Meyer-Waldeck reported to the Japanese that several persons did wish to take advantage of the emperor's offer, and next morning Captain Yamada of the investing force, with a detachment of ten soldiers, marched up to the gate of Tsingtao under a white flag, and escorted the combatants to the Japanese lines. There they were well treated and taken to the railroad, so they could go either to the international port of Shanghai or to the safety of the neutral government in Peking. Consul Peck went on to Peking to report to his superiors about the situation in Tsingtao.

Confidently, the Japanese now began their assault on Tsingtao, expecting to capture the city within a matter of hours. But instead of the lassitude they had found before, now the Japanese discovered that their every movement of troops was covered by scores of artillery shells, fired with great accuracy by the Germans. The advance began, with the British on the right wing, and it came to Litsun, where the Germans made a stand, and staged a strong cavalry charge that drove the enemy back.

For a week the forces fought each other outside Litsun, both sides suffering very heavy casualties. The Japanese did not report their dead, but they were in the many hundreds. The Germans were firing some 1,500 artillery shells daily at the enemy positions.

In this fight, *Leutnant* Pluschow's services were invaluable. Morning and night he took off and flew over the lines at Litsun, coming back to report the changes in the enemy position.

The Japanese, of course, were doing the same, but they had more difficulty, because the German positions were dug in, and some of them were quite concealed. Still, the Japanese artillery-spotting was effective, and the Germans took casualties because of it.

The fighting raged back and forth, positions and even trenches taking tremendous punishment and changing hands several times. At one point the Japanese captured a trench that had been held by the Germans for a number of hours, and found twenty-eight dead German defenders inside. After two days of such effort, Governor Meyer-Waldeck sent a radiogram to General Kamio, asking for a suspension of hostilities for a few hours so the Germans and Japanese could both recover their dead and bury them.

As the Japanese mounted this land assault that they thought would be successful in a matter of hours, at sea Admiral Kato made preparations to stage a massive effort of his own. The cruisers, battleships and destroyers headed in as close to the shore as possible and began bombarding the German fortified positions at Iltis Point and Huechuen Point. They destroyed a portion of the Iltis fort, but the Germans kept on fighting there. They also hit the Kaiser Wilhelm position with some shells. *Triumph* came in to assist in this struggle. The Germans fired back on the various ships, but the range was great, and they managed to put only one shell into *Triumph,* which caused three British casualties – the only allied casualties of the day's effort at sea.

The Japanese naval planes were used to good effect. They had established a land base on one of the little islands near the lighthouse, and from here the seaplanes could be armed with bombs and sent against the fortresses. They carried out dozens of missions on this day, and were effective in hitting the fort and knocking out some of the German guns.

The weather alternated between fine sunny October days and

dreadful storms, in which the wind howled down from the
northwest, then, as the typhoons found their birth far off in
the China Sea near the Philippines, turned around like the
dragon lashing his tail, and struck back at the coast of China.
For several days after the major Japanese assault had carried its
primary objective, storm lashed the coast and all – defenders
and attackers – ducked for cover.

CHAPTER FOURTEEN

The Breakout

Governor Meyer-Waldeck and his forces were really hardly battered by all the action that had gone before, but now they withdrew within the prepared positions at Tsingtao proper, to make their stand. And the governor put several sets of plans into motion.

On 15 October, it was decided that S-90 should make a run for it, to move outside the harbour, and through the minefield, and attack the enemy – then head south towards the protected area of Shanghai. If S-90 remained in harbour, she would most certainly be sunk or captured without doing her utmost for kaiser and country.

So *Oberleutnant* Brunner made his preparations. S-90 was brought up to the coaling dock, and the coolies loaded her with every sack of the black gold the bunkers would carry. All the ammunition she could use was put aboard. Her torpedoes were checked and the warheads made ready and attached to the torpedoes on deck, near the tubes. Finally everything was prepared, and it was simply a matter of waiting for the proper tide and time to sail when they could strike the enemy hardest.

No flag flew and no bands played that night as Brunner gave the orders and the S-90 moved away from the dock and out into the inner harbour, bound for the open sea. The orders were given for action stations, and the men went to their posts, stiff and watchful. She was alone, moving slowly in the blackness of the night before moonrise. They navigated carefully, to skirt the minefield, for it would be a bad joke if S-90 were sunk by a German mine on her way to engage the enemy. Outside, somewhere between Chalientao light and Cape Yatau stood the enemy

fleet, and it was *Oberleutnant* Brunner's task to find the fleet
and attack.

But outside, the fleet was nowhere to be seen, and then
Brunner realized that the action had been occurring north, in the
vicinity of Laushan bay, and that at least some of the enemy
ships must be there. So he turned the nose of the torpedo boat
northwest and increased the speed even in the darkness. He
must hit and run if he was to survive this night's action, for the
enemy had a dozen ships that could outgun his own, and every
one of Japan's destroyers was more modern than this old torpedo
boat that dated from before the turn of the century.

As the ship moved inshore, toward Iltis Point that had been
so badly hurt in the fighting of ships and shore batteries in the
past two days, Brunner caught sight of a large form silhouetted
against the land. It was a cruiser or a battleship, a good target
for him. Quietly he gave the orders to the torpedo officer. He
was to wait until the *S-90* got into position, and then on command was to be ready to fire his starboard torpedoes, while
Brunner executed a swift turn to port, and headed out for the
open sea and safety. Full speed ahead. *S-90* responded with a
surge of power, and swept forward. Fire torpedoes. The torpedo
officer gave the command and the torpedoes were released to
leap from the deck into the sea, and then to run beneath the
surface towards their target.

Brunner turned the ship and headed away, the *S-90* canting
over on her port beams as she moved. Then she sped off at right
angles to the enemy vessel. A minute passed and then another.
It seemed endless time. Then there came a tremendous flash of
light, followed a few seconds later by an explosion that shook
the ship. Looking back, the men of *S-90* saw the awesome
sight of a battleship blowing up and sinking in halves – the
torpedoes had apparently found the ship's magazines.

As fate would have it, the ship they had struck, the battleship
Takachiho, had been standing somewhat apart from the other
units of the Japanese and British force. The allied vessels saw

and heard the explosion too, and immediately searchlights flashed on to circle around the fleet, but so far away were the others that they caught no sight of *S-90*, and Admiral Kato came to the erroneous conclusion that *Takachiho* had struck a mine. It was a very fortunate conclusion from *Oberleutnant* Brunner's point of view, for soon he was clean away, and could set course for the cape and the open sea beyond. It was his plan to run the ship down to the neutral waters of the Huang Ho, and to take refuge in the international settlement of Shanghai, unless, of course, in the meantime he could find another way to strike the enemy.

Soon boats from the *Ikoma* and other cruisers were hastening to the wreckage that could plainly be seen in the rising moon, to take survivors out of the water. Of the battleship nothing at all could be seen save some flotsam in the water, with men swimming around it or clinging to it.

As the boats came up the rescuers could hear the Japanese sailors, singing *Kimigayo* – the Japanese national anthem – and they sang until they were all safe in the boats and on their way to the big ships.

As morning came, Admiral Kato had the count of survivors. Only one officer and twelve crewmen were saved. Twenty-eight officers and 244 men had gone down with the vessel, so swiftly had she sunk after that terrible explosion.

The loss of *Takachiho* was one of the fortunes of war, of course, but it was taken very hard by the Japanese. For although *Takachiho* was now called a second-class ship because of her age, she had been the Japanese flagship during the Sino-Japanese war, and her history was hoary with gallantry and naval tradition.

For days the Japanese and the British believed that she had been lost to a mine. Then they caught the word from Germany, for *Oberleutnant* Brunner had managed to send a message to Shanghai that had been picked up and transmitted onward, and finally the newspapers of Berlin were full of the welcome news from the Far East that *S-90* had made the *Durchbruch* from the blockade and moreover had sunk an enemy ship in the process. With some embarrassment, the Japanese and British changed their story.

Meanwhile, *Oberleutnant* Brunner and *S-90* had their own troubles. The ship was acting up, something was amiss with the old engines, and there was absolutely nowhere to take her for repairs before Shanghai. Further, the amount of traffic on the sealanes was tremendous, and every bit of it could be expected to be enemy. *S-90* had her uses, but she could not stand up against any real warship of modern vintage, and perhaps even a big auxiliary cruiser like the *Empress of Asia* could destroy her. So Brunner was forced to the reluctant conclusion that their best bet was to wreck their own ship, scuttle her and seek safety and a chance to fight again for their kaiser. They took her into the China coast, ran her on the rocks and wrecked her, destroyed everything that might be of value to the enemy, and then used the boats to make it ashore and head for Shanghai. They found themselves at Shih sueh-so, sixty miles south of Kiaochow bay. The remains of their ship were put under guard by Chinese soldiers, and the adventure of *S-90* came to an end. Unfortunately the Germans were arrested and taken to Nanking, where they were put under guard and held in internment.

The loss of face suffered by Admiral Kato and the Japanese navy could not be countenanced for long. Kato had scarcely received the word of the escape of *S-90* than he ordered new attacks on the port and every enemy vessel that could be reached by gunfire. The news from Tokyo was not good, for *Takachiho* was regarded by the Japanese as an almost sacred vessel, like the American *Constitution* or Nelson's *Victory*, with that mystical overtone the Japanese lent to revered objects. And in acting swiftly, Admiral Kato acted without as much discretion as he might have used.

For a month the Japanese and the British had steamed along

outside the line of the minefield that protected Tsingtao harbour from attack, and after a few brushes and those minor ship losses, the allies had given good care to avoid the field. They had marked the outline with buoys so they could charge down on Huichuen Point and shoot up the fortifications there. The typical attack had called for the movement of the cruisers and the battleships to the buoy line, where they anchored and fired as many rounds as they pleased at the forts.

Another buoy line was laid just outside the range of the German forts, which was about 15,000 yards from shore. This marked the point beyond which it was not safe to anchor, and in effect, the point of anchorage.

When in fury the Japanese and British moved down on the buoy line with the receipt of the news about *S-90*, they did not notice one change. German sailors, in the dead of night, had moved out to the line, following the strike at Forts Iltis and Kaiser on 17 October, and had moved the buoys in shore a thousand yards.

Next morning the cruiser force moved down with a vengeance, to try to knock out these land defences once and for all. From a point nine miles out they began throwing shells at the forts. The Germans replied, which was unusual because in the past the Germans had quickly learned that they could not reach the enemy vessels and so had given up wasting ammunition. But today they were not wasting it, as the men of *Triumph* discovered to their woe. A big shell smashed into her port side amidships, killing one man and wounding half a dozen. The orders were given, and the whole force withdrew until a new line of safety could be marked out.

Neither of these actions endeared the Germans to Admiral Kato and his staff, and their action became more stormy than ever in the attacks they could deliver, north of Laushan and from the airplanes. Almost always when *Leutnant* Pluschow went up these days he was chased by Japanese army or navy planes, and followed as far as possible by land gunfire. Only his own consummate skill as a pilot and the trusty Mercedes one hundred horsepower engine saved him.

Admiral Kato and General Kamio were becoming seriously embarrassed by the length of time it was taking them to capture Tsingtao. All the world knew that the city was defended by fewer than 5,000 men, and that its naval force consisted of old and outworn vessels, the most valuable of which had already left the harbour and sunk the battleship. So on all fronts, army and navy, the level of activity was stepped up as the commanders sought to regain face by reducing the garrison as swiftly as they could.

The increase in bombardment of the town was marked, as was the carelessness of the gun aimers. For now shells began falling all around Tsingtao and it was dangerous to move about anywhere in the city during daylight hours.

The Germans estimated now that the Japanese had more than 40,000 troops facing them in the mountains around Tsingtao. Governor Meyer-Waldeck issued orders for the defenders to save every shell and every bullet and make them all count. He had no hope by 20 October – the war in Europe had grown stagnant as he could tell by the dispatches that reached him, even beneath the caramel coating. But he was determined to fight on, and he could not but recall the words of the kaiser's personal message to him: 'God will protect you while you fight bravely. I trust in you.' That, of course, was the ruler's way of saying fight to the very end. Captain Meyer-Waldeck was determined to do just that.

In the two hotels that were now being used as auxiliary hospitals, the number of wounded kept piling up. The nursing sisters now enrolled some forty women volunteers – wives of missionaries and of officials of the German government, traders and others who chose to stay with their husbands and families rather than flee to the safety of China proper. By night the city was totally blacked out, and wardens went about the streets to see that no glimmer showed, even in the hospitals.

The weather continued to alternate between storm and sun-shine, as history and custom knew, for the saying on the China coast had always been 'September, September you will remember, October, October all is over.' The summer was gone, and the halfmoon beach around the city was covered now with driftwood and seaweed and the debris of storms.

The British-Japanese barrage became more insistent, louder and more menacing on the city. Buildings were hit, a girls' school was damaged, but there was no one in it. Fresh food became so scarce as to be a rarity – who was going to chance the Japanese armed circle around the city. Some Chinese did continue to move through the lines, the Japanese and British damned the spies who put up lights to denote positions of the artillery. But the trickle of movement into and out of the city was slighter every day.

As the anxiety of General Kamio increased, the pressure on the city was exerted again at night as well as in the daytime. From the hospital the doctors and nurses could hear the bang and crash of shells falling on the forts and in the city, and the hiss-hiss of very near misses.

Every morning the Japanese and British troops were awakened in the trenches by the sound of the Taube, as *Leutnant* Pluschow flew over the lines at dawn. Every evening the dauntless lieutenant also put them to bed, as he checked the enemy's guns and trenches before nightfall. And during the daylight hours the barrage bal-loons were up, flying above the city, to discourage the Japanese planes. For the gunners of the anti-aircraft batallions had the range of the balloons, and if a Japanese plane came near, it was subject to the hail of very accurate gunfire.

As for spotting, the balloons were not of much use, and after a narrow escape or two, the Germans took to using a stuffed dummy in the balloon basket – a lifelike figure with his glasses apparently trained on the enemy lines. But it was all a hoax, which the Japanese discovered one day when the captive balloon escaped and went whizzing out over Kiaochow bay

to come to halt at sea and be picked up by a destroyer. Until
the report was in, the Japanese wondered what kind of trick
the Germans were up to now.

In the city the coal resources of the *Shantung Bergbau
Gesellschaft* were concentrated and protected as much as possible
from fire. Many of the volunteers who had streamed into Tsingtao
from Tientsin and Peking were employed as firemen and policemen to allow the old firemen and policemen to fight in the
lines.

A hiatus in the attack was forced by nature during the last
week of October. Storms as severe as those anyone could remember smashed the city and the surrounding hills, and made a
quagmire of the no-man's-land between the trenches of the
Japanese and British and the German defences.

Japanese headquarters was located at Tchang-tsun, and on
the rare occasions when the sun showed during this week
Leutnant Pluschow was sent out on his scouting mission, which
included a flight over Japanese headquarters to see if it had yet
been moved. In he came, to whizz above the thatched roofs of
the Chinese villages and draw rifle and machine-gun fire from
the emplacements around the camp.

The Japanese placed their siege guns atop Prince Heinrich
Hill, and made ready for the assault on the city itself. It seemed
to the allied correspondents who had now been allowed to accompany the Japanese army that the sons of the Rising Sun were
moving like sleepwalkers in their attempt to capture Tsingtao.
There was a reason for it: back in Tokyo the Okuma cabinet
was facing a crisis brought about by its ambitious entry into the
war against the wishes of some older statesmen who wished Japan
to be as independent and isolated as the United States had
chosen to be. The war party, which was Okuma's, was interested,
then, in presenting the *fait accompli* of the capture of the German
colony at just the proper moment. With some 60,000 men now
in the field, plus a fleet of warships, the task did not look very
hard.

The breakout of *S-90* and the sinking of *Takachiho* could be regarded as an accident of war. As far as naval forces were concerned it must be the end of it for there was not another ship in Tsingtao harbour capable of breaking out of the port.

CHAPTER FIFTEEN

Days of the Siege

The spirits of the Germans trapped in Tsingtao were raised considerably by the reports they had from home and abroad about the activities of their cruiser squadron. On 12 August the cruiser *Emden* had arrived in the Marianas to meet with the other ships of the East Asia cruiser squadron, and there Captain von Müller had secured permission to go raiding alone in the Indian Ocean.

Admiral von Spee and the rest of the captains of the squadron had no illusions about the eventual fate of von Müller and his ship – nor did the doughty captain. A single German ship entering a British lake could not expect to survive for very long.

She would be unable to make use of Tsingtao base. She would have no coaling stations open to her. She would have to become a buccaneer and steal her provender where she could, then use it against the enemy as long as she might stay afloat.

Emden steamed down through the Dutch East Indies then, and made her way into the Indian Ocean. In August, as the men of Tsingtao awaited the word of Japan's attack on the city, *Emden* was resupplying and coaling from a German collier on the edge of the Indian Ocean, and dodging the British heavy cruiser *Hampshire* which was out looking for her.

When the fighting on the edge of the colony began in September, the soldiers were cheered by word that a raider had appeared off Colombo and sunk and taken several ships. Then early in October came word that a raider had insolently attacked the British port of Madras and burned the Standard Oil tanks there. Later that month the raider had terrorized the seas round Rangoon and the entrance to Calcutta, and attacked French and Russian warships in Penang harbour, sinking the Russian cruiser *Yemtschuk* and the French destroyer *Mousquet*. This was indeed great news for the beleaguered defenders of Tsingtao.

For a long time they heard nothing from von Spee, except that in September the squadron had wrecked the British cable station at Fanning Island, and bombarded the French colony at Papeete.

On 27 October, as the winds blew wickedly and the rain came down in sheets to pelt the defenders and attackers at Tsingtao, Admiral von Spee and his cruiser squadron were in passage around the wildness of Cape Horn, listening to the signals of the British cruisers *Glasgow* and *Good Hope* that they knew to be somewhere in the area. On 31 October, the cruiser squadron was steaming up the South American coast towards Valparaiso, where von Spee intended to stop for supplies. In Tsingtao the city began to shake and the hills around it to reverberate with the sounds of British and Japanese field guns. The final assault on Tsingtao had begun that morning, directed by General Kamio from his brick headquarters at Chang Tsun. The foreign correspondents were allowed to go up on to Prince Heinrich Hill, where fifty brave Japanese had lost their lives in the assault not long before, there to observe the progress of the fight against the city.

The Japanese were always good at picking celebrated occasions for optional activity – in this case the assault might have begun on 1 November, but was hurried a day so it could be started on the anniversary of Emperor Mutsuhito's accession to the Throne of Heaven. That looked very good in the newspapers and added face to the Okuma cabinet to be so thoughtful.

How *Leutnant* Pluschow ever made it through the smoke and flame that arose over his city no one would ever know, but precisely at dawn, as usual, the whirring throb of the Taube's Mercedes could be heard, and the little plane appeared out of the clouds, circled, and returned along the firing line towards Tsingtao.

Within an hour the siege guns struck their first important target: they hit the big oil tanks down along the inner harbour, where fuel oil and gasoline for the vehicles was stored. Fortunately for Pluschow, Captain Meyer-Waldeck had ordered the airplane's gasoline supply to be stored elsewhere in fifty-gallon drums, and most of the gasoline in the tanks had been emptied. But the oil tanks were full and they blazed very satisfactorily, while atop Prince Heinrich Hill the staff officers and correspondents stared through field glasses at the thick clouds of smoke that rose over the beautiful European city.

From the hill, Japanese General Kamio and British General Barnardiston had a fine view of the whole operations area. Off to the left in the Yellow Sea, outside the dangerous line of the minefield, they could see the Japanese and British force of warships, steaming back and forth, bombarding the shore installations along the harbour. They could also see that line of buoys, so carefully laid by the British, and then so craftily moved by the Germans. Below to one side stood the remains of the handsome Meckler house, burned by the Germans on their retreat into the city, and here the Japanese had established a field battery that was now adding its thunderous output to the sounds of siege.

Directly below them in the gathering sunlight, the generals could see the old *Kaiserin Elizabeth* in the middle of Tsingtao harbour, gathering steam to go over as close as possible to fire on the Japanese positions in the hills. Off to the right was Bismarck fortress and the coastal forts were on all sides in front. Further to the right were the Japanese and British camps and the zigzag line of the trenches that had been so important before Prince Heinrich Hill was captured.

The guns flashed and smoke came from their muzzles. In the town could be seen the great clouds of bluish-white smoke that indicated an exploding shell.

The huge tanks of Standard Oil and the Asiatic Petroleum company first smoked blackly, and as the fires gained control they began to blaze with golden and yellow and red flame. The fuel spattered out on to the naval godowns nearby and these too began to burn. The firemen rushed out from their company headquarters, with their firetrucks, to save the naval docks if possible.

From the top of Prince Heinrich Hill that morning, the officers and correspondents had a grand show. Soon the warships opened up on Fort Iltis with everything they had, and on Fort A, which jutted out on the peninsula to Huichuen Point. The German siege guns at this point were big and dangerous as they were at Iltis. They were built right into the rock, and when they fired they rose up out of the rock, their long barrels glinting in the sun, fired with a mighty explosion, and then sank back in recoil beneath the surface. Where their shells struck, the observers could see big gouts of water rising around the ships. But the ships moved briskly so they might not be sitting ducks for the excellent German marksmen.

Behind the hills, along the railroad the Japanese engineers worked to restore the line, so that flatcars loaded with shells could be brought up to the siege guns. Teams of horses and wheezing trucks crowded the roads, bringing more supplies for the siege. General Kamio had determined that this time the fight would be carried to the finish the Germans had promised.

All day long the guns thundered. From the German side the firing was much less impressive, for Captain Meyer-Waldeck's men had been cautioned to save their ammunition. They fired when they had something to shoot at, and they knocked out several Japanese field pieces that day. But mostly the defenders 'took it', for the barrage laid down by the Japanese and English was overwhelming.

Leutnant von Plissow and other naval men found themselves on horseback, riding along the defence lines of the city, moving men here and there to dig in and man the guns and the field pieces that kept the enemy from overrunning them. All day long the scream and crash of shells dominated the city, concentrating on the barracks and the fortresses, for these places where the field guns spoke up were the major target of this first day's work.

The guns also worked over the harbour installations. The coaling dock was set afire and its godowns began to smoke with that heavy grey vapour of burning coal. The 150-ton crane on the edge of the great harbour was hit by a shell from a siege gun, and the whole upper works disintegrated. In a moment only the base was standing there, awkward and broken, hanging to one side.

Fort Iltis took a tremendous beating. Great hunks of stone were torn away, revealing the steel reinforcing rods of construction. The steps and stairs fell to big armour-piercing shells, and men died as the guns were hit. In mid-afternoon one of the big steel siege guns suffered a direct hit, half a dozen men were flung about as ninepins, and the gun was silenced forever. Later, towards the end of the day, as the sun began to move towards the horizon, a second Iltis gun caught a shell from one of the cruisers offshore, and its breech was blown out.

As the sun went down, the warships at sea began to retire further out, for who knew what devilry the Germans might be up to. It was possible that they could sneak out in small boats and attach mines to the ships. It was possible that one of their warships could be made into a missile and sent forth, like the fireships of the past, to wreak havoc by explosion.

So the Japanese and British cruisers and battleships retired and the harbour was quiet.

Over on the land front, the Germans sought the coming of the shadows to make a desperate counter-attack. As the sun dropped behind the Pearl Mountains, out of the depths of Moltke fortress came a short armoured train, charging along the tracks towards the Japanese installations. The train skirted the bay of Kiaochow, and then stopped. Half a dozen guns began spitting fire at the British installations on the right, smashing 37 mm and 75 mm shells into the twisted trenches of the enemy. Then, after ten minutes firing, the locomotive started up again, and reversed, and pulled the armoured train back inside Moltke fortress.

That night, as the Japanese and British commanders met to plan the next day's work, the sappers were busy in the trenches, extending them, rebuilding where the armoured train had done its damage, making new trenches that zigzagged along the contour of the land, three feet wide at the bottom and four and a half feet wide at the top. It was a bitter night, and the rain came down to turn the fields before them into a sea of grey mud, to fill the bottoms of the trenches with three inches of muddy water, to pelt the men and keep them from sleeping.

Out at sea the Japanese and British warship commanders met, and it was agreed that next day *Triumph* would concentrate her tremendous firepower on the forts on Bismarck Hill. These were potentially the most dangerous to a ground attack.

In the town, Captain Meyer-Waldeck assembled his defence forces. From the port came the word that the old gunboat *Tiger* had caught a shell that smashed away most of her tall smokestack, and made her very much a relic. So that night the sailors of *Tiger* moved the old gunboat out to the edge of the outer harbour and sank her, so that she might become an obstruction that would one day catch one of the Japanese or British cruisers as they came into the port.

That night, too, *Leutnant* Pluschow conferred with the governor. From now on it would be impossible for him to fly the Taube again. The Japanese and British had zeroed in on his field, they had placed their guns now only four thousand yards away, and their accuracy and intensity of fire was such that he did not believe the Taube should be used except in one last emergency. The governor agreed, and ordered Pluschow to prepare for that one emergency. For when the time came, the Taube would fly again.

So the first day of siege ended in a pouring rain, the chill winds of the north driving down to remind Japanese and Englishmen as well as Germans that whatever the affairs of men, nature still ruled.

CHAPTER SIXTEEN

2 November 1914

At dawn on 2 November, the allied barrage began again. A hundred guns opened up on the forts as the sun crept across the edge of the mountains. Smoke rose up with the mist and the men in the trenches rubbed their eyes and sat up to await what came next.

For the Germans it was to be another day of punishing shelling. That first night the sappers had extended the trenches towards the German positions, but there was still a good 750 yards of no-man's-land between them.

This day the Japanese artillery found the electric power station and damaged it beyond the ability of the Germans to make repairs under fighting conditions. So from this point on there was no power, and the people at night had to depend on gasoline and kerosene lamps for light.

All three of Tsingtao's harbours had suffered heavily in the shelling of the past few hours. The coaling station was badly damaged and fires still smoked in the godowns. Holes had been smashed in the concrete quays, and the rail line that led down to the naval quay was broken in several places. The floating dry dock had been hit and was canted over to one side – not that it was needed, for the only ship of any consequence still afloat in Tsingtao harbour was the *Kaiserin Elizabeth*.

The Chinese city behind the European port was virtually untouched. The Germans had been thorough – everything of value to Europeans in Tsingtao had been concentrated in the German city. So the Chinese – those who were left – could go about their business almost unbothered by the shelling. But most of the Chinese who were left were kept in virtual slavery by the Germans who needed them and their services more than ever. The rickshaws had disappeared from the streets with the first shells, but the hand-drawn carts still moved about transferring supplies and even personnel from one point to another.

Iltis fort had suffered severely in the shelling of 1 November. Once there had been six twelve-calibre guns, two ten-calibre and five nine-calibre guns in those revetments, carefully protected from enemy fire. But the concentrated efforts of field guns and the cruisers and battleships over a twenty-four hour period seemed to have reduced all but a few to broken pieces of metal.

Bismarck fortress remained almost unscathed. Its guns were trained north against the land invaders. Its defences were divided into two sections, one containing twenty one-calibre guns and machine-guns. The second section contained four twenty-eight-calibre guns which looked out over the seacoast, and these guns were still dangerous, potentially able to sink the *Triumph* or another battleship.

Moltke fort had been sorely hit and its kitchens and laundries and other self-contained equipment were somewhat battered.

Down below, on the harbour, not too much attention had been paid to the Tsaichen battery and Huisingchao battery on the outer harbour. These consisted of a number of guns in turtleback turrets of steel and concrete. Each turret stood on a platform which could be raised or lowered into the ground and covered over. Each position was also equipped with several searchlights that could disappear at will. Today they were to receive the attention of the sea forces.

Triumph concentrated her fire on 2 November on the Bismarck fort, and her big guns rang out time after time, sending shells that pierced the steel and concrete coverings of the fortress and exploded below. They were devastating in their destructive power and within an hour after beginning shelling, one of the big guns was knocked out.

The British and Japanese took heart because the Germans had nearly stopped firing their guns. Intelligence reports came to General Kamio to the effect that the devastating fire of the ships and batteries was knocking out the German guns. The truth was that Captain Meyer-Waldeck's men were almost out of ammunition.

The rain and cold had made a morass of the front lines that existed on this day. That whole front measured five miles, with the British headquarters located plump in the heart of the muddiest spot in the valley. The officers' mess consisted of a single round table with a hole punched out of one rim by a shell, half a dozen chairs and some empty provision boxes – all this out in the open. The whole was surrounded by shell holes not further away than twenty yards. On the left three Japanese batteries of 75s blazed away at the German forts endlessly, while on the right ran a line of bivouacs for officers and men, made of sticks, twigs, mud and stones, with roofs of tarpaulin. The whole appearance might have welcomed a caveman, but few others. And inside lived some six hundred Tommies and Sikhs, who moved out of the bivouacs before dawn and threaded their way into the trenches to fire their Enfields at anything that moved up on the hill.

The Japanese fire was heaviest against Tai tung Chien and by the afternoon of the second day the mountain seemed to have developed smallpox, so heavy was the concentration of shellholes and circles of fresh dirt thrown up. One after another the German light gun positions were destroyed. No machine-gun, nor earthen work could stand up under a hail of 75 mm shells for very long. This day was given over largely by the Japanese to reduction of the advance positions at the bottom of the hills so that the trenches could be moved forward during the night.

The same treatment as the day before was meted out by the ships, concentrating their fire on the forts, and passing Iltis fortress once again. When Iltis did not reply, the Japanese believed they had knocked it out but the fact was that the big guns had run out of shells.

But while Captain Meyer-Waldeck and his defenders were

fighting a battle they knew to be hopeless on the Tsingtao front, they were immensely cheered by the news from Europe and from other German war fronts. The news of the battle of Penang was out – a thoroughgoing victory for Captain von Müller in sinking two allied warships and one of the most daring acts of the war. *Emden* had captured another British ship or two, which was not yet known, but it was very apparent that the British had the wind up in the Indian Ocean – even the Asian press was full of it.

In Europe the Germans had captured Lille, and were moving against Ypres; they had captured St Mihiel and forced the British out of Antwerp. German and Austrian forces had marched into Poland and were planning a great offensive to knock the Russians out of the war before winter.

On 1 November, von Spee and the East Asia cruiser squadron suddenly appeared off the South American coast opposite Coronel, or Santa Maria as it was sometimes called. Here they were about 150 miles southwest of Valparaiso when they ran across the British in the form of the cruisers *Glasgow*, *Monmouth* and *Good Hope* and the auxiliary cruiser *Otranto*.

Immediately the call to action was sounded – *Klarschiff zum Gefecht* – and Admiral von Spee made ready to fight his enemy.

Good Hope was the flagship of Admiral Cradock, the indefatigable commander who had very nearly captured the cruiser *Karlsruhe* in the opening hours of the war, and who had been working day and night since to clear South American waters of German raiders.

The result of this meeting could have had only one ending: von Spee with his two big armoured cruisers and three light cruisers engaged, Admiral Cradock chose to fight, and *Monmouth* and *Good Hope* were destroyed – only *Glasgow* and *Otranto* escaped. It was a naval victory to impress all the world, and when Admiral von Spee steamed triumphantly into Valparaiso harbour on the morning of 3 November, the world learned the details. Nothing could have been more vitalizing to the morale of the defenders of Tsingtao than to learn of the victory of their very own squadron.

On 3 November, the British and Japanese ships appeared off the city as usual; this day *Kaiserin Elizabeth* was no longer there steaming bravely back and forth in the harbour, to lob shells when she thought there was a chance of hitting an enemy. She had fired all her shells on the afternoon of 2 November, and learning this, Captain Meyer-Waldeck had given the fateful order: that night the Austrian cruiser was taken out to the edge of the harbour and scuttled in a strategic spot near *Tiger*, where she would hold up any big enemy vessels trying to make it into the port. All the guns and all useful things had been taken from her the night before, all had been stored in the undamaged godowns, and *Kaiserin Elizabeth* had shuddered as the seacocks were opened and the water poured into her bowels to take her down among the fishes.

On 3 November, the allied officers directing the battle assembled on Prinz Heinrich Hill once more to watch the awesome bombardment. General Kamio was becoming nervous with the amount of time it was taking to reduce these German fortifications, and the tempo of the firing increased for a while until nature intervened. The clouds came sweeping in from the northwest over the mountain, and soon the gunners could not see to fire. It would do no good to send up the observation planes to direct the fire, for the cover was as heavy over the German city and the German forts as it was over the allied positions. There was nothing to do but sit and wait, huddled in great–coats atop the steaming mountain. The storm had struck at 1100 hours, and it raged around the peaks, halting the war of men, until 1400 hours when the clouds suddenly blew away. In the thickness and the mist, the Japanese engineers had been busy: they had moved their trench line another hundred yards closer to the Germans, and soon would be on top of them if they did not move back. The Japanese batteries moved forward too in the cover of the storm that was better for them than

E

darkness. Their forward battery had advanced past the Mecker house to the village of Ta Pau, half a mile closer to Tsingtao.

The afternoon, then, brought the most severe fighting of the siege so far. The Iltis fort ran completely out of ammunition and the guns shut down. The Japanese pressed hard against the German hills, and the German big guns were not often heard, for their shell supply was very low. The defenders fought with grenades and machine-guns and rifles.

On the sea, the silence of Iltis allowed the cruisers and *Triumph* to come in as close as they dared in view of the continued existence of the minefield. They did come in and they bombarded the city and its defenders from the sea front.

As the sun fell even the brightening news from Valparaiso was eclipsed by the stern facts of Tsingtao's situation. The Japanese had launched an attack late in the afternoon and overrun the front lines, because Fort Bismarck could no longer lay down a barrage to stop them. They had captured some twenty-six field guns and eight hundred men during the day. It was a serious blow to the defence of Tsingtao.

On 4 November, the barrage opened up again with renewed fury, and all day long the Japanese and British guns pounded at the city and the forts, receiving hardly any return fire. There was almost nothing left to shoot, and Governor Meyer-Waldeck had warned his commanders that all they could do was loose an occasional shot to let the enemy know they were still alive.

For some reason General Kamio believed the Germans were lying doggo and would rise up when the final assault came and throw a whole new barrage against his troops. He might have attacked with his infantry on 4 November, but he did not. He continued to bombard with fury all day long, and the Japanese planes flew over city and fortresses unopposed except by small arms fire.

The Japanese had time now to work out some military innovations. They began to use the wireless as a means of sighting in the guns of the naval force. The ships stood offshore, but they were unable to mark their shooting properly. So a naval station was established at the back of the Japanese lines, and in a protected position several marine officers were stationed with telescopes focused on Iltis and the other forts. One of the ships would fire on cue, and one of the marines would telephone the exact location of the burst on a grid-iron map. Aboard the ship the gunners had exactly the same maps, marked out in the same way. When the spotter's word was wirelessed to the ship, the gunners knew in a moment where their shell had landed and could correct to be more accurate.

Now that the Germans were giving them so little trouble the Japanese could do the same on land. They ran up an observation balloon from Prinz Heinrich Hill and the observer with his telephone line did for the ground troops what the marine observers were doing for the ships just off the harbour. It was all very leisurely and very accurate – and bore little relationship to war, being more like a turkey shoot or a grouse hunt.

On the extreme right of the lines, where the fortress trenches ran down almost to the bay of Kiaochow, the firing was very heavy. The Japanese and the British under General Barnardiston were pressing hard on the German lines in front of Moltke fort. General Johoji was the Japanese commander here; his men fought so bravely and pushed so hard that they came up to the fort that guarded the pumping station for the city. Johoji was an intelligent commander. He knew that he could blow up the pumping station but he also knew that if he did so, when they took Tsingtao they might well find the city a mass of typhoid and cholera because of it, and that the saving of a bit of time on this end could cost thousands of Japanese and British lives as well as German. So the detachment approached the fort and surrounded it. Then the garrison inside the stone fortress was warned that unless they came out the door would be dynamited. And if that were done, and survivors were not killed in the fighting, then the pumping station might be destroyed to the detriment of all. The German defenders were as intelligent and humane as the Japanese – the door opened and twenty-three German naval men and volunteers stepped out to the ignominy of surrender.

4 November was the crucial day. And the surrender of the fort at the pumping station was the crucial surrender, for it gave the Japanese a foothold between Bismarck and Moltke forts, and exposed the flanks of both to fire.

It was a dreadful day. General Kamio in his headquarters at the base of Prinz Heinrich Hill kept to his dugout, studying maps, listening to officers and talking on the field telephone while he sipped warming tea. Mid-morning the general had the welcome news that a dozen new twenty-eight-centimetre siege guns had just arrived in the field and were being zeroed in from positions at the rear line near the railhead. Soon their sound was unmistakable all along the line. They exploded with a tremendous bang, but that was not the most characteristic of their sounds: the immense shells, whirring through the air, made a noise like a giant skyrocket going off, and the explosion when it came was louder even than the heaviest of the German siege guns.

The Japanese were not unscathed, nor were the British and the Sikhs. Stretcher bearers moved along the lines, with their bloodstained canvas racks, sometimes folded, sometimes heavy with a covered body, perhaps an arm dangling down as the men of mercy took the wounded back to the field hospital behind the trenches.

On the German side, the hospital on the hill had been abandoned as unsafe and the emergency hospitals in the Prinz Heinrich Gasthof and the other hotel were overflowing with wounded by the end of the day. The wounded came in by stretcher, by ambulance, by cart, from the fortresses and the lines. The nuns were out in the forts helping to bring home the wounded, the doctors were working in their bloodstained smocks, cutting and sewing and cursing war that turned men into bloody bits of meat.

And down in the town, at the headquarters, Governor Captain Meyer-Waldeck was receiving the reports from all his fighting fronts, and preparing to make the decisions of the night so that his slender and dwindling force could be used to the best advantage on the day of horror he knew must dawn in a few hours.

Of the four thousand men remaining to defend the city and its fortresses, some two hundred were just boys. Most of the rest were volunteers, for Meyer-Waldeck had lost a large part of his regulars in the opening days of the siege when the warfare on the northern slopes of the fortresses was at its height.

Each fort was defended by about two hundred men, no more, although the garrison possibility for each was four or five times as high. The old planners had envisaged the attack properly, the new administrators had not been able to support the force necessary to beat it off.

In the forts there were still sixty guns and a hundred machine-guns, but the ammunition was almost gone. Some criticized Meyer-Waldeck for wasting ammunition, but the fact was that his officers were doing the best they could to hold out as long as they could, and nothing else.

CHAPTER SEVENTEEN

Tsingtao's Last Day

On the night of 4 November, the snow began to fall over Kiao-chow bay and the land beyond, and soon the trenches were little lines of zigzag depressions against a broad field of white. The snow stuck and piled up that night, and the wind blew and howled and drove the snow into drifts against the barbed wire and the sandbags.

The men of both sides huddled around charcoal fires, while the men at sea in the ships put on their foul-weather gear and winter mittens if they had to go on watch, and slapped themselves and stamped their feet to drive away the cold.

All night long the white of the snow and the dark of the night was emphasized by the yellow flashes of the Japanese and British artillery as they prepared for the infantry's work of the next day.

That night, Captain Meyer-Waldeck ordered the reserve ammunition to be sent out to the forts, and starshells went up over the field. The Japanese had come almost to the edge of the fortifications, the word had been passed that evening to the captain, and now he gave his orders. The starshells illuminated the field, and the forts began firing shrapnel for the first time. Until this day the Germans had held their slender supply of anti-personnel shells, and had kept their guns firing at the enemy pieces and ships and the locomotives that brought war supplies up along the rail line. But this night it was so desperate a situation at the foot of the hills that Captain Meyer-Waldeck brought out his reserve weapons.

From Fort Moltke and Fort Bismarck came five, ten, fifteen, twenty shrapnel shells, then the firing stopped and the searchlights stuck their long white fingers across the field, seeking moving men. They found them, passed, and came back, to illuminate a dozen Japanese sappers, sandbagging a new trench. Another starshell illuminated them, and the machine-guns opened up, sending the rattle of their death signals along the line. Men threw up their arms and fell, and others tumbled down into the trenches to escape the hail of death.

Then another starshell, more searchlights to probe the field and determine the movements of the Japanese and British, and the rattle of machine-guns, and the pop-pop of the anti-aircraft guns turned low, and the crash of the shrapnel.

All night long the darkness was punctuated by flares and searchlights, and the firing kept up. Beyond the hill, Captain Meyer-Waldeck's marshals for once had no difficulty in maintaining the blackout, for the city was in Stygian darkness, with the electrical power system gone.

On the morning of 5 November the shelling began early on both sides. Before the sun had been up for an hour the Tsingtao forts were veiled by a cloud of smoke and dirt from the scores of shells that fell on the slopes.

That morning General Kamio was talking openly about his final assault on the fortresses. It would come at night, he said, either this night or the next in all probability. He expected that he might lose an entire regiment in the assault.

The British were not pleased with this attitude towards losses, and Captain Shaw, one of the staff officers, told Jefferson Jones, an American correspondent, that he hoped the Japanese would change their minds. But there was not much chance of it; Japanese and British methods of infantry warfare were a million miles apart. The British took the position of professional soldiers; all their men were enlistees who had joined the colours of their own volition years ago, and come to garrison Tientsin and Weihwaiwei. The Japanese in this army, almost without exception, were conscripts scarcely trained, and the officers used them as cannon fodder. Their part was to overwhelm a position by

numbers and to hang on until more of their troops could come
up and the artillery could silence the enemy beyond. It was a
very expensive but a very quick way of warfare.

Late on the afternoon of 5 November the Japanese and British
warships began to close on the city, coming in more daringly
than at any time since the sinking of the two destroyers
and minesweepers at the beginning of the naval action.
The disappearance of every German naval vessel encouraged
them in this.

That day, Governor Meyer-Waldeck sent for *Leutnant* Pluschow, who made his way down from the airfield where he was
waiting helplessly, moving the decoy Taube around. It had
taken any number of hits in the past few hours, but the loyal
Chinese workmen took the broken wood and nailed and glued
it back together again every day, so it still looked like an airplane.

The whole city was now hard hit by Japanese and British
shells, and many of the streets were pocked and the sewer and
water lines broken in places. Coming down from his mountain,
Leutnant Pluschow had to be careful not to wreck the car, but
finally he pulled into the courtyard and ascended the grey stone
steps that led into the administration building.

The governor greeted the lieutenant cordially. In the past
few weeks Meyer-Waldeck had learned a grudging respect for
the airplane and the man who flew it. Now he had one last task
for Pluschow to perform.

The Japanese would overwhelm them soon. That much was
certain. Meyer-Waldeck was a student of Oriental methods, and
he knew how General Kamio planned to finish this action. The
Japanese were bound to succeed when they came, because the
garrison no longer had anything with which to fight except a
handful of shells that would be exhausted in a few hours.

They could hold out until the morning of the sixth, Meyer-
Waldeck had assessed the situation and was sure of that. Early
next morning, then, Pluschow was to take off from the racecourse airfield and make his way into neutral Chinese territory,

where the last dispatches of the colony would be delivered into the hands of the nearest German consulate.

Meyer-Waldeck looked straight at his subordinate and asked him what he thought of it. Pluschow was surprised, there was no question about that – these were orders and he would carry them out. Did he really think he could make it? asked the governor. He doubted personally if the Japanese barrage would let him through. Pluschow set his face – he was determined to make it, he said.

So Meyer-Waldeck shook the lieutenant by the hand, wished him good luck, and sent him on his way to spend the rest of the day preparing the Taube and anything else he planned to take on the trip he was to undertake.

Pluschow went back to his quarters, and packed up the handful of things he could carry with him, then went up to the airfield to wait through the long hours until nightfall. There was absolutely no chance of doing anything to help the situation during the day, for the moment the Japanese spotters in the hills saw the slightest movement around the airfield, they plastered the area with shells, and tore up the landing and take-off space some more.

During the afternoon, Pluschow had a fine show from his airfield seat. The Japanese-British fleet came in close enough to be seen clearly, and began the first real naval bombardment of the city proper, from behind Cape Jäschke.

They shelled the great houses on the beachfront without mercy, and Prinz Heinrich Hotel, although it was being used as a hospital. Sister Lena and the doctors began moving the patients out of the place, down into the basement of the hotel and other buildings nearby.

Darkness finally came, and with it a let-up in the accuracy of the enemy fire, although not in the intensity of it. And as darkness fell, Captain Meyer-Waldeck knew the Japanese would advance against the fortresses, so he saved the last of the shrapnel. The emergency lighting system had exhausted its resources by

E*

this time, and the searchlights did not work. Instead the Germans used starshell to light up the battlefield, and these rockets went up every few minutes, to explode and hang in the air, revealing in cold light the events below. They found the Japanese worming their way ahead, under the hammer blows of the shrapnel from the German guns. Dozens of men fell, but the stretcher bearers carried them back and others took their places, until by daylight the Japanese had advanced another two hundred yards.

Dawn found the battlefield a wretched painting by a cruel nature. The snow had begun pelting down in the middle of the night, had changed to freezing rain, and then to a downpour as the temperature rose. The trenches were ankle deep in water, and where the water was exposed to the blasts of the gale, it froze into ice. For the wind was blowing at forty miles an hour in off the Yellow Sea that morning, the thermometer stood at two degrees below zero in General Kamio's camp, and the wind-chill factor in the trenches brought the simulated temperature down to around thirty degrees below zero on the fahrenheit scale.

In the intense cold of the dawn of 6 November, *Leutnant* Pluschow found it very difficult to start the frozen engine of the Taube. All night long the Chinese and his enlisted men had worked with pick and shovel and barrow, filling the potholes in the airfield made by the enemy's rain of shells. In the hangar, Pluschow made sure his propeller was dry and well glued for this last flight, and the Mercedes was heated with oil pots so that it would start at the right time.

Just before dawn, the plane was wheeled out onto the field in the darkness that covered and prevented the spotters above from seeing the movement. Pluschow followed the plane to the field, put on his flying helmet, and shook hands all around with his workers and mechanics. They knew they would not see him again during this struggle.

Then he jumped on to the wing and clambered into the cockpit, a mechanic spun the propeller to catch the magneto, and after a few sputters the Mercedes caught and began to turn over with a blue-white exhaust. He taxied down to the end of the field with the wind, and turned back to take off upwind, over the jagged rocks at the end of the runway's dropoff.

As he taxied, the flame of his exhaust caught the eye of some spotter in the hills behind, for as he got off the runway and began to rise, the enemy placed a shell so close behind that the plane was knocked upwards by the draft of the explosion. As he gained altitude he circled once, and in the dawning saw his mechanics below waving to him, and the red, white and black of the German Eagle flag over the hangar where it had flown for so long.

The cold at ground level was intense – up here in the un-sheltered cockpit, in his thin clothing, he was nearly freezing, but that did not matter to him. He had Governor Meyer-Waldeck's last reports and dispatches and he was determined to deliver them safely somewhere in China. He headed west.

Pluschow had talked over his flight plan with others and had decided to head west to Haichow, about 150 miles northwest of Tsingtao, well out of the Japanese range of influence. But as he rose in the sun, and looked about him at the countryside, he saw a grey muddiness to it that distressed him. Outside the fighting area he dropped down, and his fears were confirmed, the untimely autumn rains had left the whole flat plateau here a sea of mud, and landing was bound to be difficult if the terrain did not change markedly. Three hours went by, and he had used up three-quarters of his fuel. He came to Haichow and found the flood conditions as bad here as anywhere. There was no dry ground on which to land. Even the roads were streams of mud.

He went on then, searching for a dry landing place. Another hour passed, and his gasoline supply was almost exhausted, so he turned back, and found a field that seemed to be a little dryer than others, and headed down.

It was an illusion. The plane's wheels touched the ground,

then sank into the heavy wet clay up to the hubs and over, and the undercarriage struts caught, and the Taube pitched forward on to its nose, smashing the precious oaken propeller to bits and throwing Pluschow out ignominiously into a soft, sticky bed of mud, where he landed with a loud splash.

Immediately, out of the mud came a crowd of Chinese in their blue and black pyjamas, to laugh at the foreigner in the mud, and then help him up and brush him off as he scrambled back to the plane to secure his precious papers. He found them, and was turning about, wondering how he would ever communicate with anyone who spoke decent German, when he was addressed in English by a voice. Looking up in surprise he saw a European – or rather an American – for it was a missionary named Morgan who lived near Haichow, and who had observed the plane in its distress and come out by motorcar along its track.

Mr Morgan then took *Leutnant* Pluschow in tow, arranged with the local warlord to guard the Taube, and hustled the German officer and his papers into the motorcar. First he took Pluschow back to his house for a bath, clean clothes and breakfast. Then they drove to Haichow, where Pluschow delivered his papers and told the consul the sad story of what he knew of the last days of the colony at Tsingtao.

This cold wet weather was unusual even for North China so early in the season, and the men had not been issued winter clothing. So there they were in cotton uniforms, without great-coats, standing in the frozen mud in the trenches – no galoshes or mud boots, no mittens, none of the fur coats and warm clothing that were issue in the Japanese and British armies for winter weather. All they had to warm them were the fires they might build from charcoal if they could find it for there was not a stick of dry wood in the vicinity. They were frozen and shivering and frostbitten, and still they persevered against the Germans, who were relatively cosy in their warm uniforms and close quarters of the fortresses.

That day General Kamio made the decision that the attack would come next day, and so the barrage was stepped up, although many would have wagered that it was impossible to increase the rate of shelling. All afternoon and into the night the shells screeched across the no-man's-land and into the sides of the fortress mountains.

As night fell, the activity around General Kamio's headquarters was stepped up. The general was eager to learn the precise state of his attacking forces and that of the defenders as far as intelligence could guide him. Staff officers trickled up to the front lines to confer with line officers, and wrote down in their notebooks what they learned, then came back to report to headquarters.

The Japanese and the British had advanced by mid-evening to a point just twenty-five yards from the stone wall that skirted the fortress line for three miles, from the bay of Kiaochow on the right to the Yellow Sea on the left.

A few yards behind the front line troops massed the second line, and behind them the reserves. Behind all stood the siege guns that smashed at the walls and German weapons all day and all night with their tremendous shells.

The night of 6 November was a repetition of the night before. The Germans knew the end was not more than hours away and they expended starshell and shrapnel with an abandon that would have seemed reckless a few days before. Here was the scene as reported by correspondent Jones to his newspaper, the *Minneapolis Tribune:*

Starshells continually fired from the German walls would burst in the heavens above and for several minutes would keep continually lit the field below. Japanese infantrymen would be seen outside fresh trenches placing sandbags and the like, and with darkness covering the field again there would be a few seconds of deathly stillness and then the machine-guns along the redoubt walls of the Tsingtao forts would open up. From all about the field in front there appeared the bright red flash of flames as field and siege guns went into action, and the echo of their deep roaring undertones would at length subside into the ripping pom-pom-pom of the German machine guns as they attempted to check the advance of the Japanese sappers. . . .

At around midnight, the starshell stopped illuminating the terrain between fortress and the trenches. For an hour there was almost dead quiet. General Kamio began asking why, and he sent word to General Yamada, in command of the front, to discover the reason.

CHAPTER EIGHTEEN

Surrender

When Governor Meyer-Waldeck heard the intense quiet descend on the battlefield behind the city, he was not surprised. He knew why the fire of the fortresses had come to an end. For as he had been expecting for hours, the guns had run completely out of ammunition. Now, Meyer-Waldeck and his officers and men had fulfilled their duty to the kaiser – they had defended Tsingtao to the last shell bullet in those big guns.

What would happen now?

That is precisely what General Kamio wanted to know. So General Yamada sent out several scouting parties. They moved to the slippery, clay- and mud-filled trenches just below the German redoubt, and they climbed to the top and over the sandbags in the darkness. Ahead of them there was no sound at all.

Over the wall, the men made their way, and dropped down ten feet. Before them ran a whole tangle of barbed wire emplacements with no breaches in sight – but also no German troops to fire at them. By telephone the scouts called back to ask for spares and reinforcements, and then lay down to wait and listen. No sound came to them. The enemy had disappeared.

Half an hour went by, and then the sappers came up with their heavy gloves and wire cutters and began snapping away at a segment of the wire. Soon one tangle was loosened, and then another, and by 0100 hours General Yamada and three hundred Japanese soldiers made their way through the wire and were inside the central redoubt of the German fortress.

On the right the British began to advance, doing just what the Japanese were doing, not knowing that directly ahead of their position was stationed a detachment of two hundred Germans, armed with rifles and machine-guns and a considerable supply of ammunition, determined to fight to the last man.

The British moved on, and the Germans began lining up their guns. Suddenly through the night came a loud command in Japanese, off to the right and rear of the Germans. The German lieutenant in command started like a deer in an alfalfa patch. He gave a quick order, and the Germans rose and hurried back into the shadow of the fortress.

At all costs they must avoid being encircled and cut off.

But instead of reaching safety, the Germans ran into a hornet's nest of Japanese fire. General Yamada and his men were ready. They were on one side of the German defenders, and the British Tommies were on the other. Both fired on to the mass of men, killing and wounding more than half of them.

Within half an hour the positions known as Forts 2 and 3 were captured, and then General Hoiruchi on the left took forts 4 and 5. General Johoji moved forward, and General Barnardiston did too, but they did not move far. For the remaining troops of the garrison were concentrated at these positions and Johoji and Barnardiston ran into heavy fire as they tried to move up.

Barnardiston saw that he could not make a frontal assault. As dawn began to send its fingers along the ridge, he also saw that his men could move along the sides of the high-banked macadam road that the Germans had built to run from Litsun to Tsingtao. Knowing of the perennial flooding, the German engineers had been very thorough, and had built well and high, with many culverts to drain the heavy rock underlay. The road ran at right angles to Tsingtao's redoubt, the steep sides of the road gave good cover to the men, and they advanced along the bottom on both sides until they reached the wall, then the sappers came up and blew a hole in it, and the British troops were inside to capture their fort.

Half an hour later before the sun was properly up, General

Johoji was engaged in a firefight at his fortress line, and by 0630 hours that, too, was taken and the Germans were pushed back all along their front.

The defenders now moved back to Forts Iltis, Bismarck and Moltke, which stood about a quarter of a mile behind the redoubt that was now in enemy hands. Generals Horiuchi and Yamada continued to advance, and there was very little that the defenders could do to stop them, for they had no big guns ready to answer back when the Japanese siege guns sounded.

On they came, and behind General Kamio spoke to General Yamashita, and the whole of the Japanese reserve was committed to the action. On they came through the breached lines, until 17,000 men were assaulting the slopes of the German garrison mountains, and now fewer than 3,500 defenders were left to answer back with rifle and machine-gun fire.

As the sun found the crevices of the hills it glinted down on the guns of the Germans and the bayonets of the advancing Tommies and Japanese.

The allies had to cross an open space three-quarters of a mile wide, and begin climbing the slopes of the three fortress mountains if they were to take the city from behind. They fought their way up, until the defenders saw the sea of men in grey and brown and khaki before them and saw how hopeless was the plight of a garrison that did not have a gun larger than a machine-gun with which to defend against these thousands that poured through the breaches in the line.

Back at his headquarters General Kamio listened to General Yamashita, who spoke on the telephone, gave brief orders, and turned to inform his chief. General Kamio was smoking a cigar and coaxing his pet parrot to eat breakfast. Here is a report from the scene that day:

Near by was a crowd of Japanese newspaper correspondents, hastily scribbling telegrams, an officer giving them details. Telephones buzzed and receivers clinked. Then two companies of infantry appeared along the edge of a gully, descended into it, and piled their arms. Every now and then an orderly was called up and given precise instructions, after which he saluted, mounted and rode away.

On the slopes of the fortresses the Japanese charged upwards, and as they came the machine-guns began to rattle. The Japanese came on in waves, the guns cutting them down by the score but soon one way shielded another and it was a matter of numbers – 3,000 men could only hold out for so long against 17,000.

The end came at 0705. It was indicated by the running up of a white flag near Governor Meyer-Waldeck's palace, and then other white flags on the fortresses. The governor had decided to stop the slaughter before all his men were killed.

CHAPTER NINETEEN

Japanese Victory

Within the hour the flag of the Rising Sun appeared atop every fort and every major public building in Tsingtao, and the red, white, and black flag of the Imperial German government was never again to fly over the Asian mainland. In the city and among the victorious Japanese troops it seemed a scene of happy tranquility – even the German officers and men were unruffled, and some of them seemed almost not to have known there had been a battle.

But appearances were deceiving as any who visited the shoulders of Moltke and Bismarck knew. For the dead of both sides still lay on the slopes, Japanese and British and German blood mingling in the cold day's sun. The Japanese began rounding up the soldiers, and collecting arms. They improvized a prison camp at the foot of Prinz Heinrich Hill, territory they knew well by now, and which they had converted over the past weeks to their own.

General Kamio accepted the surrender of Captain Meyer-Waldeck, and the Japanese general had the courtesy to refrain from staging a victory march through an enemy city. Instead, all the German officers were given the freedom of the city, and the Japanese soldiery were kept completely out of the city itself. They were quartered at the Moltke and Bismarck barracks at the rear of Tsingtao, and so were the British Tommies.

For the next ten days, then, General Kamio made ready to take over the city, the colony and the administration of this Chinese territory.

The Germans had done a good job of blowing up and destroying things of value that the war had not wrecked. On Iltis fort the guns were destroyed, but mostly by the Germans, not the Japanese. Much had been made by the correspondents of the fleet's destruction of the guns on Iltis. Now the allies learned that what they had destroyed were wooden replicas some two hundred yards from the real guns, that *Leutnant* Trendel, who in peacetime was manager of the Grand Hotel des Wagons Lits in Peking, had tricked the allied naval forces, and had blown up his own guns only when surrender became imminent.

The great surprise to the Japanese was to discover that the German guns were almost all intact after their days of bombardment, that the real damage to the forts was done by the Germans after they ran out of ammunition. The Germans had also brought up guns from the various gunboats and other vessels which were stripped for the war effort. The guns that were 'blown up' or captured largely belonged to an ancient era, and were leftovers from the siege of Paris in 1871. The modern guns were kept deep underground and protected and remained that way.

When the end was near and it was obvious that the garrison must surrender soon, the Germans brought up nitroglycerin sheets and wound each gun muzzle in them, then stuffed dynamite plugs into the barrels. Only at the moment of actual surrender were the guns fired, and destroyed as neatly as a child splits his wooden gun muzzle with a knife.

Everywhere in the forts and barracks, all items of equipment that could be usable to the enemy were destroyed. In the post office all the German stamps were burned. In the godowns the leftover canned goods – fish, meat, sauerkraut – were opened and left to rot so that the Japanese and British might not enjoy them nor would they help in any way to further the enemy war effort.

Pluschow had been given his secret papers to deliver, and other agents had been sent through the enemy lines with other papers. Still others were burned so that when the enemy came, the secrets of fortification, the building plans of the public buildings, the sewer plans and all that would be of use to any administrators were destroyed. When the Japanese got Tsingtao they got only the shell of a city.

Two days after the surrender, correspondent Jones was allowed inside the city, and this is what he saw:

The city appeared as if a typhoon had passed through it. Its wide asphalt and macadamized streets, fronted by beautiful four- and five-storey buildings of German architecture, were vacant. Giant shells, some three feet long and a foot in diameter, were lying about on sidewalk and street still unexploded. Trees, splintered at their bases, lay toppled over in the avenues. Windows in the houses were shattered, while gaunt holes in the sides of buildings, where shells had torn their way, made the residence blocks appear to be gasping for air.

Out in the harbour could be seen the spars of the (merchant ship) *Rickmers,* and two or three other German freighters which had been sunk at the opening of hostilities about the city, while farther out in the channel was the grave of the Austrian cruiser *Kaiserin Elizabeth,* which had been sunk by the Germans.

The whole scene seemed one of devastation. Streets deserted of people, showfronts of stores completely gone, as was also the merchandise, harbours deserted of ships, and not even a sign of a rickshaw to remind you of the Orient.

The battle was over. Tsingtao had fallen.

CHAPTER TWENTY

Taking Over

The Japanese and British were jubilant with the capture of Tsingtao because they had lost so few men. Much credit for this must go to the exuberant charges of the Japanese on the forts.

Iltis fort had been guarded by sixty German soldiers, with the thought that if the fighting got hot they could call back for reinforcements stationed below the fort, and have help within half an hour. But when the Japanese assaulted the hill, they came up so fast, in the face of machine-gun fire, that they overwhelmed the Germans before the reinforcements could arrive, and the commander just had time to blow his guns.

Bismarck and Moltke forts had been taken the same way. The casualties on the hills were high, but in all the Japanese claimed to have lost only 1,700 men dead in the fighting. Meyer-Waldeck was surprised – he had figured the loss at five thousand at least.

As for the naval actions, when it was all over, the strategists asked Governor Meyer-Waldeck for his assessment. He was particularly qualified to give this assessment because he had grown up in the naval service. He was not very well up on the Japanese naval strategy or tactics, but was on the British. *Triumph*, he said, had comported herself by the highest naval standards all through the action, and had been as effective as she could possibly be.

But what Governor Meyer-Waldeck held his highest praise for was the conduct of the Japanese and British artillery on the points behind the hills. The rain of fire they poured into the forts was so devastating that no man dared leave the trenches and start a counter-assault that might have thrown the enemy back at one point. Moreover, the rain of death continued hour after hour and day after day, said the governor, as he was questioned.

The Japanese and British victors were kind and thoughtful of their enemy as they prepared for the transfer of power. There was no march through an arch of triumph, nor any embarrassment of the Germans. Symbolically (in retrospect) the transfer of power came on 11 November, 1914. All the enlisted men of the German service were rounded up and moved to a nearby seaport in the north, from where they would be transported to Japan and go into prison camps. A number of line officers, who were needed to spot the land minefields in the trench area, were kept back for that special duty. All were assembled one last time at Moltke barrack on the morning of 11 November, and paraded for Meyer-Waldeck at roll call.

Then came the sound of marching feet, and the musical noise of men whistling in unison. Up over the hill beyond the barracks, where the muddy road dropped down below the crest, suddenly appeared a troop of men in khaki, guns at their shoulders, with bayonets attached, and khaki sun helmets glinting brown in the morning light. They came in fours, nine hundred of them, the men of the British Expeditionary Force, the borderers, the old pros, and they were whistling in lieu of a band to accompany them. Their tune was *Everybody's Doing It*.

The Germans blenched as they passed, for never before had they seen the sight of foreign soldiers tramping along their road as conquerors. No sooner had the last Briton turned down the hill, into the city, than the Germans, too, burst into song – and theirs was equally fitting – *Ich hatt' einen Kamerad*. And they sang it loudly and with poignancy to the very end.

Then the officers and men shouldered their packs and duffel, shared out some cigarettes among them, and at an order from Meyer-Waldeck, they moved out, without guard, headed for the port and prison.

It was five days more before the Japanese were ready to take formal command of Tsingtao. How would they look if the toilets would not flush or the water system failed? All that had to be settled in the transition period.

All day and night the engineers checked and worked, and down on the Strand, where the Europeans had disported themselves at the beach clubs and where an oriental was never, never allowed, they put up a wooden monument that looked much like Cleopatra's needle, the obelisk that stands on the Thames Embankment in London.

And then on 16 November, the formal ceremony was held. General Kamio was in the reviewing stand in the middle of the city. The troops passed and headed for the monument. General Kamio and his men disassembled and reassembled there.

On both sides of the obelisk stood huge straw-wrapped casks of sake, and piles of cigarettes and food, all surrounded by chrysanthemums – sacrifices to the souls of the heroic dead who had made this moment possible.

When the troops had assembled in the square, facing the monument, General Kamio stepped forth, bearing a large scroll. The troops uncovered their heads, and so did he. Then he bowed deeply to the monument, and opened the scroll, and began to read:

I, the humble General Kamio, commander-in-chief of the Japanese forces, express my hearty condolences to the souls of the dead who have been killed in battle or who have passed away from illness contracted during our days of war. . . .

It was a Shinto ceremony, calm and simple, and it took only a few minutes. Then he finished, rolled up the scroll, handed it to an aide, and received a pine branch in its place. He bowed again, stepped forward and placed it at the foot of the obelisk.

In a way strange to the westerners it was a brave and impressive ceremony. Afterwards, the Japanese unbent – they invited their British allies to formal entertainments, and the officers all dined together at the Bismarck barracks officers' mess that so recently had belonged to the Imperial Germans. For two weeks, the British troops remained in Tsingtao, having the freedom of the city, while cautiously the Chinese residents began to return to a place the Japanese promised would be quiet, where wages would be high, and there was to be no more mistreatment than the Germans had allowed. Then, after the two weeks, the British troops embarked on the *Triumph* and sailed for Hong Kong, where they boarded troopships and went back to the more serious struggle in France. General Barnardiston had led an historic force of nine staff officers, 910 non-commissioned officers and men of the 2nd Battalion of the South Wales Borderers, and 450 non-commissioned officers and men of the 36th Sikhs. They had distinguished themselves as they would again, losing twelve killed and sixty-one wounded, while the Japanese lost hundreds.

The removal of the mines at sea and on land was the most ticklish of many operations undertaken by the Japanese. Some fifty Japanese officers and men were killed in the next few weeks in taking up the explosives on land, largely because the tremendous bombardment of the field had pushed mines around, buried some, and generally made the minefields into wreckage.

But finally the clearing was accomplished and the city and colony could settle down.

Governor Meyer-Waldeck, who was formally appointed an admiral by his kaiser in the last days of the siege, received the Iron Cross and other medals, as did many of the Germans, in absentia. They were sent to Japan as prisoners, but in view of their gallantry the emperor permitted them to keep their swords.

General Barnardiston was invited to Tokyo as a guest of the emperor, and was fêted royally there for a week. The Japanese gave him the Order of the Rising Sun, second class, and his chief-of-staff Major Pringle was awarded the fourth class order, while his adjutant, Captain Moore, was awarded the fifth class. Then they left Japan to join their men again.

All this occurred in the last days of November 1914, and the early part of December. Tsingtao had fallen, and the German presence in East Asia was no more. As if to add emphasis to the whole change, on 8 December, Admiral Graf von Spee's East Asia cruiser squadron, the pride of Tsingtao, was found by Admiral Sturdee's searching squadron of cruisers, destroyers and auxiliary cruisers, and in a battle as hard and swift as that of Coronel, the German squadron was scattered and destroyed. So the end came almost in a package.

CHAPTER TWENTY-ONE

The Repercussions

Scarcely had the Japanese taken control of Tsingtao when Britain and the other allied powers began asking when Tokyo intended to return the old German colony to China. The answer was never if she did not have to, and as late as possible if she did. The Japanese war party intended to conquer China, and here was a heaven-sent foothold.

At home the Japanese government had its troubles, and in the few weeks following the seizure of Tsingtao, even that event did not aid Premier Okuma's government.

In China, the Japanese seizure of Tsingtao was greeted with considerable woe, for the Chinese knew which nation really threatened their territorial integrity. After the Sino-Japanese war and the loss of Korea and Formosa, the Chinese knew only too well what to expect.

At the time of the fall of Tsingtao, the Japanese population of the city was less than 1,000. Two years later, it amounted to 2,300 and in 1918, when the war ended, the Japanese had swelled their resident population here to 24,000. This was partly an indication of increased Japanese business activity in Shantung, and partly an indication of the Japanese push to bring people to China to establish the colonial foothold they wanted so badly. They established schools, added to the hospital and created a medical school. They took over the coal and iron mines.

When the time came, at the end of the war, for them to return the land to China, the Japanese showed their hand. On 18 January 1915, the Japanese had presented their famous twenty-one demands on China to President Yuan Shih-kai. Those demands virtually ensured the Japanese control of the area, of its railroads and of the control of Manchuria and Inner Mongolia. They went so far as to demand that the Chinese use Japanese banks, that the Chinese should not cede any more territory to countries other than Japan, that they employ Japanese 'advisers' at every level of government and business, and that Japan be given a free hand in all ways in China.

With the coming peace in Europe, the western powers were far more concerned with events and situations in Germany and Central Europe than they were in Asia, and Japan then secured the control of the old German colonies in the Pacific that she had wanted for so long. She also managed to get some of her Chinese policy in line, although France, Britain and Russia had enough strength in China to resist and encourage China to resist the most outrageous of the demands. Yet anyone in the world who might wonder what the Manchurian incident of the 1930s and the China war of 1936 was about, could have discovered the whole truth by re-reading the Japanese demands of 1915, made just a few days after the fall of Tsingtao, and planned out long before the collapse of the German government there.

As war came to an end, the Chinese came back to Tsingtao and to the battered area of Kiaochow. Soon the population of Shantung was over 30,000,000 people, and they began to prosper under Japanese influence. So it was not entirely a one-way affair.

In 1917 the Chinese declared war on Germany, not really because China had any quarrel with the Germans, but because the government of Yuan Shi-kai feared that unless the Chinese could come to the peace conference table with strength, they would never get their territory back from Japan. China was more successful than many at home had hoped – once again it was a matter of the self-interest of the various powers.

After what seemed to be interminable diplomatic negotiating, in the summer of 1922 all seemed ready for the return of the Chinese territory of Tsingtao to China, and in December of that year it was done, on paper at least. There were all kinds of complications: who was to own the International Club? Who owned the grounds of the Commercial University? What was going to happen to the Golf Club?

But China got the big wireless station and the German-built government buildings, and the nominal control of the rail lines. Japan did not let go but she kept her rail interests (as opposed to *control*) and she kept salt and mining and trade concessions — any trained observer could see what Japan was planning.

But on the surface it looked good for the Chinese and it appeared that they were beginning to win back the colonies that had been wrested from them with so much warfare, hurt and bitterness.

Then Shantung became truly Chinese and in the next few months was overrun by warlords. Chiang Kai-shek managed to restore a certain loyalty, and stop the kidnappings and rape of the area, but Shantung was only under nominal control of the Kuomintang government. And that was what was wrong, both before the famous incident of the Marco Polo bridge and the days at the end of the Second World War when Shantung, peaceful as she was when the United States marines occupied the territory, rapidly succumbed to the pressure of Mao Tse-tung's armies.

It was not until the success of the Chinese revolution in 1949, that Kiaochow and Tsingtao really settled down to become Chinese entities. And even today, one who visits Tsingtao will see the wide bay and the old German buildings that were constructed to last a hundred years. They have already outlasted three regimes.